TRANSFORMING LIFE INTO LIVING:
A GUIDED WORKBOOK FOR TAKING
CONTROL OF YOUR LIFE

Transforming Life into Living Series

Mary Jo McCabe
&
Dr. Bhrett McCabe

Authors and Publishers Disclaimer

This workbook and all related publications were written and produced to provide information and commentary on the subject matter presented. This workbook does not take the place of any professional, psychological counseling or other consultative services, and the reader should not construe any professional relationship as a result of purchasing this publication. Should professional services be warranted, competent professional agents and services should be sought.

ISBN 0-9708088-5-2
Retail Purchase Price: $18.95

The Psychic and The Doc Radio Program is a production of The Psychic and The Doc Radio Program, LLC. It can be heard on radio stations throughout the Southeast on Saturday evenings or online at www.thepsychicandthedoc.com.

Cover design by Jacquie Hotchkin, Dedicated Business Solutions, Inc.
www.netdbs.com.

TABLE OF CONTENTS

INTRODUCTION

Life is meant to be lived. Nothing more, nothing less.

The demands of our life are increasing and it seems more and more likely that in order to succeed in life, we must be more efficient and effective at managing these demands. With new technology, cell phones and email, we are constantly in touch with our loved ones, but we are also continuously connected to work. This is a dramatic shift from our ancestors who communicated through letters, personal visits, and even the sharing of telephone lines. Even though their demands were dramatically different than what we face today, they were, nevertheless, stressful and consuming. Their demands were dramatically different than what we face today, albeit stressful and consuming in their time.

Consider the life of our loved ones just 100 years ago. Those involved in farming would awaken at the first break of sunlight and work the farm until the sun went down. Their work was physically demanding since they were not assisted by the modern technologies we are so accustomed to today. There was a routine to their day. Their personal stressors were as real to them as the ones we face presently, but the difference was that typically at the end of the day, their work was done until the first break of sunlight the next morning.

It was not uncommon for their evenings to be filled with family time, family dining, or family activities that encouraged relaxation, such as reading, going to church, or engaging in a hobby. Those working in cities such as bankers and business owners experienced different stressors than the farmers, but similarly, when their day was over, they returned home and spent time at home decompressing. How does that compare to your life?

The modern technologies we depend on to function more efficiently in life are often at the root of our problems. These technologies are similar to the Spy Ware you download on your computers. You do not realize that they are working behind the scenes until you realize that your computer is running so slowly that you now have a major problem. Our modern conveniences seem so easy and helpful that you have no idea that your life is about to hit a wall, slowing down to a moment of inefficiency and a feeling that you need to reboot your life. They are slowly eroding at the quality of your life, and the result is that life begins to demand all you have to give instead of you demanding all that life offers.

The problem arises when we lose the balance and perspective of who we are in life. Without warning, a time comes when we are forced to take account of where we are in life, and the results are staggering. Unlike our ancestors, work demands answering emails, completing spreadsheets, and researching on the Internet well into the evening hours. Communications between friends, families, and loved ones are now more than ever, fragments sent via text messages, instant messages, or email. It is increasingly more difficult to disconnect because we are so dependent on being connected. The Spy Wares of life are slowly and insidiously wearing you down until life informs you that you need to reboot.

Now is the time to reboot. Life is meant to be lived and you are the one that must do the living. Too many of us are being lived by life, and it should be the other way around.

Living is an active process that requires all of our resources directed at the target to be successful. When life is in charge and takes on the role of a dictator, your resources are exhausted and overwhelmed. You miss the times to recharge emotionally, physically, and spiritually. What you feel now is not how you will feel when you take back control of your living. Unfortunately, you have felt this way for so long, you have forgotten what it means to live life on your terms the way that you want to live.

Through this workbook, you will learn to understand the influence that our thoughts, our feelings, our reactions, and our behaviors have on living life. They are under your control, created by you for you. For example, turning off the BlackBerry and other devices in order to enjoy family time in the evening or even to engage in personal meditation is asserting yourself as the boss and puts you in control. You set the boundaries and expectations for growth, but you have to accept the most important challenge of all – A Willingness to Put Forth the Effort for Change.

If there were only one way to approach life, we would all be living the same way, using the same tools, and the conflict and stress we all feel would be nonexistent. That being said, we make life and the way we live it so complicated that sometimes the greatest thing you can do is slow down and take account of yourself. We do not need to wait for a major event or personal upheaval to force us to count our fingers and toes. We hope that through the teachings, exercises, and reflections in this workbook you learn the importance of understanding who you are, what drives you, and what is truly important in the daily events in your life.

We started this journey to bring you a reference to change the way you approach life, but to do it in a manner that was different from anything else. It is only fitting that it is in a workbook format because life is truly a workbook full of chapters, exercises, challenges, and most importantly, reflections. This workbook is the first of our new series of interactive and introspective workbooks that will challenge you through the teachings of The Guides and impact you with activities from us, The Psychic and The Doc. The result is something that we are proud of and hope that it will impact you the way that it has impacted all of us who have worked to put this together.

This workbook is the first resource that contains unedited teachings from The Guides. Many of the teachings have been collected from previous workshops and seminars, but never released in a format such as this. Although the language of the readings may appear difficult, they were received and transcribed through tranced teachings. As you become familiar with the dialect of The Guides, it will become easier to interpret the teachings as they were given, free from the influence of our interpretation. Our family has been greatly influenced by the teachings of The Guides, and we want you to feel the same way as you transform YOUR life into living.

Now is the time to accept the challenge and start living life the way it was meant to be lived…

"To change your life, believe in you. To believe in you, wonder about you. To wonder you must have confidence, you must have serenity, but more importantly, you must be satisfied with the choices you make for you."
—The Guides

CHAPTER 1:
LIFE

"Life is truly a book of memories. Memories that must be kept secret from you
until you are past the hurdles of life that are lived through while here on Earth."
—The Guides

You are the most important person in your life. This approach is not a new perspective, as investment advisors will tell you the same thing about investing your money. Every financial planner shares the same philosophy, to invest in self at the beginning of each month before paying any bills. This approach ensures that your investment will be made before squandering the money on less meaningful pursuits, and help make you a better investor if you follow that advice. From the way you approach the world to the way you perceive yourself, making the most out of your life depends on how well you know you. You have needs and wants that guide you, but you must trust the balance that will help you achieve the needed balance between your spiritual growth and your physical desires. Needs are important for you to achieve your wants. You must understand the difference.

The following teaching from The Guides expands on this perspective as it shares insights on how to view experiences of your past as teaching points for the path and journey you are walking today. Understanding the importance of your past and the experiences that you have gone through will help you gain the peace you desire and the control over your life that is important to *Transform Your Life into Living*. It is simple; you must believe that it is as simple as The Guides teach.

A Teaching from The Guides...

From our world there are many who guide you. Through life's lessons, we help you learn how to balance your life both emotionally and spiritually. Working through the lessons you encounter and overcome physically, you find your true self, your soul. Once you touch your soul, it becomes easier for you to accept the past, embrace the present, and await the future.

When you are uncertain of your life's path, you become fearful because when you look outside of yourself, life seems foreign. Your life will always seem foreign if your life does not begin within yourself, and even though fear can be a healthy emotion it must not rule your world. You must understand the need of fear in order to understand the gift of it.

Once you accept the responsibility of your life, you then understand the importance of it. In order for you to live a peaceful life, you must become aware of your emotions, why you react the way you do to life's songs. You must understand the importance of time, as well as learn how to be in control of the life you live today.

You see life is what you perceive it to be. When your life is always difficult, you grow accustomed to it. It then becomes hard for you to change. Until you change, your life will never seem peaceful.

What is important for you to realize is that a peaceful life begins when you no longer look at the world as a challenge, but rather as a tool to nourish your soul. When this shift happens, you understand that life has a purpose. The power of this truth helps you to live peaceful in your world.

To live peaceful is to connect to you spiritually. What we mean by that is to honor you in what you are, who you are, and the importance of the path you walk today.

When you touch your soul, you then see life from a different perspective. The things that you thought were important no longer have meaning for you, and you begin to understand the need for honesty, true honesty. No longer do you lie to yourself about what you feel or what you need or want, for it is then that you truly understand the reasoning of your own mind and the choices that you have already made. As you look back on all the choices that you made, you become honest with yourself about what motivated you to make those choices, and the needs that you were seeking to be met. It is important – so listen! Because when you do listen, you realize that every song sung and every script written have all been different journeys to teach you about you. Look at it not only on a physical level, but also on a spiritual level. See the bigger picture of it.

When you begin to truly be honest with yourself about your life, then you are no longer afraid to face you, you are free to embrace you. Then life begins to have meaning and you are no longer afraid to face who you are, and you can see the bigger reason for why you live your life.

To live peaceful means nothing more than to stay in control of your environment and not complicate your life with dishonesty. Sometimes you may look in the mirror and you see a face you do not know. When you are living in a realm of dishonesty about what you need and want from yourself and others, you only create for yourself heartache and disappointment.

This is why challenges in your life are never met. This is why things that you feel you want never have gain because you are lying to yourself about why you want them. Understand you are not lying to yourself about wanting it - you are lying to yourself about "why" you want it.

Look at yourself today and know what it is you strive to have. Then, ask yourself honestly why you feel you need it and why you want it. This is all to make your life better. When you bring other people in your world, regardless of whether they are friends or more family, it is to make you feel good about you, it is to make you feel complete. When you are able to be honest with yourself about your needs, you are then able to reach the success that you want.

Regardless of the needs you may have and the successes you want, there are three things that are important at all times of your life, and they are: dignity, integrity, and freedom. In understanding these three things, you will not be affected by the hardships of life that others experience. Good day.

Now it is time for your interpretation of this teaching. In the following section, please summarize your thoughts and the impact that this teaching might have on your living. Each teaching has different meanings for each of you, so this section is truly personal to you. Throughout the "YOUR INTERPRETATION" sections, we included provoking and challenging questions to assist you in achieving the meanings and impact for you.

YOUR INTERPRETATION:

_____

_____

_____

_____

_____

_____

_____

_____

_____

_____

_____

_____

_____

_____

_____

_____

_____

_____

_____

_____

_____

_____

_____

_____

_____

_____

_____

_____

_____

_____

_____

_____

_____

_____

_____

_____

_____

_____

_____

_____

_____

_____

_____

_____

_____

_____

_____

_____

_____

If you were going to take one message away from this teaching that would help you describe it to a close friend, what would it be?

_____

_____

_____

_____

_____

_____

_____

_____

_____

_____

_____

_____

_____

_____

_____

_____

_____

_____

What does it mean to live peacefully in your life? Reflecting on your life, how does this compare to how you are currently living?

_____

_____

_____

_____

_____

_____

_____

_____

_____

_____

_____

_____

The Guides share that every experience in your life has a purpose, and that you must have control of life to achieve the peace you desire. How can you live free by maintaining the control of your emotions?

_____

_____

_____

_____

_____

_____

_____

_____

_____

_____

_____

_____

_____

_____

_____

_____

_____

What do you NEED from life to have the life you desire? What is necessary for you to be a fruitful and successful individual? Try not to create a grocery list, but challenge yourself from the perspective of what you feel is important in you, your capabilities, and your qualities that you need to live the life you want.

_____

_____

_____

_____

_____

_____

_____

_____

_____

_____

_____

_____

_____

_____

_____

_____

_____

_____

_____

Put the items in the description you provided above in the order of greatest importance to you in your life, RIGHT NOW:

_____

_____

_____

_____

_____

_____

_____

_____

_____

_____

_____

_____

_____

What do you STRIVE to HAVE from life? This is not a goal setting activity, so try to focus on what you feel that you want from life to be successful. There are no guidelines since you are the only one who truly knows what you want out of life at this point.

_____

_____

_____

_____

_____

_____

_____

_____

_____

_____

_____

_____

_____

_____

_____

_____

_____

_____

_____

_____

_____

_____

_____

_____

_____

_____

_____

_____

Do your NEEDS and WANTS differ? Are they the same?

Not many of us truly understand the differences and similarities of those aspects of our life that we need to be prosperous and those for which we strive. The truth is that many of us were taught at an early age that our wants and needs should come after the wants and needs of the family, organization, or relationship. Following this logic, the demands of others outweigh our personal pursuits. Unfortunately, this is an overly simplistic perspective that stunts our own growth and pursuits and one that fosters feelings of guilt.

We want you to picture a tree in the middle of the forest. This tree is rather large, with long extending branches that invade the space of other trees. Underneath the tree, there are smaller plants, flowers, and ground cover, all bunched near the base of the trunk. Like the long branches, the roots of this tree extend across the floor of the forest, mostly underground out of common sight. What is the role of a tree that has reached this magnitude in the forest?

The truth is the role of the tree is much larger than we can understand. The first impression is that a tree of this magnitude is keeping water and other vital nutrients from reaching the smaller trees, ground cover, and plants. We may look at the tree and think that its needs have been overtaken by what it strives to want – water and nutrients. Fortunately, the forest and many of the other ecosystems of our world work in better harmony than humans do.

Trees in forests work in conjunction with each other. Trees of this magnitude have long, extending branches and roots because of their need to collect water and nutrients. They need the water to grow large and to provide shelter and other nutrients to smaller plants, trees, and ground cover that simply could not survive without the larger, more imposing tree. Consequently, what looks like an overly aggressive tree in search of its own needs, is in truth a tree that knows what it needs in order to provide for others. Most importantly, the tree understands its place and role in the ecosystem, and strives to maintain this balance so others may live.

Your NEEDS and WANTS are just as important. It is not a negative to understand what you need and want from life so long as you understand that the balance in life should be maintained. You cannot contribute to those around you unless your needs are fulfilled and your wants are addressed. But as The Guides pointed out in the teaching, your needs and wants in your life must be honest to create the peace you desire.

What do you feel stands in your way to achieve what you WANT and what you NEED from life?

WANT:

_____
_____
_____
_____
_____
_____
_____
_____
_____
_____
_____
_____
_____
_____

NEED:

_____
_____
_____
_____
_____
_____
_____
_____
_____
_____
_____
_____
_____
_____

Limitations in life serve many purposes. Think of them as signs on a highway. Some have greater meanings than others. A double yellow line and a *Do Not Enter* sign mean more than a sign that says *Slow Traffic Stay Right*. Life is no different. You encounter limitations in your life all the time. You must be able to recognize what they are and what their purposes are before you begin to take action. You can choose to ignore the sign, like many of you who choose to ignore the speed limit sign only to risk being handed a ticket. When your choice is to ignore those signs, you must know that there may be consequences. What are these limitations trying to tell you? Are you paying attention to these limitations?

Of the limitations that you have identified, examine whether or not they can be addressed, changed, or simply heard but requires no action. Most importantly, try to identify why these limitations are in your life:

_____

_____

_____

_____

_____

_____

_____

_____

_____

_____

_____

_____

_____

_____

_____

_____

_____

_____

_____

_____

_____

_____

_____

_____

_____

_____

Sometimes, we have to understand what we can change and what we cannot change. We spend so much time on aspects of our lives that we cannot change and overlook those parts of our lives that we can change. We become exhausted and frustrated, allowing aspects of our lives we cannot change to define who we are. Unfortunately, it is not reality. It is a perception that we allow to become us because it is safe and familiar.

You are not the best evaluator of yourself. You are much better at highlighting the strengths of your closest friends than you are at finding your own strengths. In fact, try and recall a time when you were supporting a close friend through a difficult time, a break up, or a loss. What do you usually focus on? You highlight the positive aspects of your friend, trying to make him or her feel better. Why can't you do that to yourself? The truth is that it is difficult to do…until now! Complete the next exercise to understand your own personal strengths.

What do you feel are your strengths, your assets, to help you achieve:

WHAT YOU STRIVE TO HAVE?

_____
_____
_____
_____
_____
_____
_____
_____
_____
_____
_____
_____
_____
_____
_____
_____
_____
_____
_____
_____

WHAT YOU NEED FROM LIFE?

_____
_____
_____
_____
_____
_____
_____
_____
_____
_____
_____
_____
_____
_____
_____
_____
_____

Looking back at times in your life and the difficulties you have experienced, how have they been impacted by your NEEDS and WANTS? Select one time in your life when you were not honest in your NEEDS and WANTS and examine how that impacted you. What was the outcome and how could things have been done differently?

_____
_____
_____
_____
_____
_____
_____
_____
_____
_____
_____
_____
_____
_____
_____

_____

_____

_____

_____

_____

_____

_____

_____

_____

_____

_____

_____

_____

_____

_____

_____

_____

_____

If you chose to live your life all over again, what two qualities about you would you want to bring with you?

1. _____

_____

_____

_____

_____

_____

2. _____

_____

_____

_____

_____

_____

Why did you select these qualities?

_____
_____
_____
_____
_____
_____
_____
_____
_____
_____
_____
_____
_____
_____
_____
_____
_____
_____
_____
_____
_____
_____
_____

You can learn a lot by the qualities that you value within yourself. For a variety of reasons, they have become your strengths, the values that you treasure within you. When life becomes difficult, it is easy to overlook these qualities and place greater value on those that are not as important. It is a common misperception but one that can be avoided. View your own strengths much the same way that a business would view their assets, as components to build around. When an organization has unique assets, they work to market and differentiate themselves from their competition. You are no different. You embody qualities that are specific and unique to you. See them as assets to value and assets to market.

EXERCISE:

Imagine that you are standing on the very top of a hill. Look at what lies in front of you and then see yourself turn around to see what lies behind you. Now you need to make a decision on which direction you choose to go. Which direction are you drawn to? You can either walk down the hill in front of you or turn around to walk down the hill behind you. Which way do you walk down the hill?

INTERPRETATION: Restructuring your life

In front of you – You like the way your life is going. Even though you might want to have things better, you have no intention of changing your life.

Behind you – You are extremely practical. However, you need to work on erasing old behaviors in order to search and find new life. You allow yourself few choices because in your mind, what worked once can work again.

EXERCISE:

Are choices hard for you? Regardless of what you think, let's see how your soul sees it. Try this exercise: Imagine that you are planning a vacation to an unknown city. You have choices as to what you want to see and do while you are there. Do you opt to see the same tourist spots that others go to see, or are you more inclined to venture off into the side streets to see the local spots?

INTERPRETATION:

If you chose to see the **tourist spots** without venturing off on your own, you like to go with choices that feel safe. Choices are made for you. Perhaps choices aren't as easy for you as you might think. This isn't to say you don't have choices. It just means it's harder for you to make choices. You analyze or go back and forth on choices you have made.

If you chose to **go off on your own**, you like to make your own choices about things. You don't want someone else doing it for you. You make quick choices and usually stick to the plan you create.

Be aware of your attributes and your strengths. This chapter has reinforced this thought, but it is something that you must continue to maintain in your daily approach to life. Through this understanding, you will better understand your purpose, your needs, your wants, and most importantly, what drives you to be you.

CHAPTER 2:
DIGNITY, INTEGRITY, & FREEDOM

"To live an honest life, be aware of what you really want. Look at the things and the people in life that give to you joy. Look at the people in your world that give to you pleasure. Seek truth that brings satisfaction to you, that inspires you, that gives you a purpose for belonging, for those are the things of life that truly are of value." —The Guides

In the previous chapter, The Guides briefly introduced the concepts of dignity, integrity, and freedom, and their importance in your achieving success. Each of these concepts contributes to you living a life of honesty, a concept that has been a core feature of The Guides' teachings for many years. According to The Guides, living a life of honesty is your gift of appreciation to God for the privilege of living on earth in the world of man.

The following teaching shares the role of dignity, integrity, and freedom in your life. Each requires a balance to foster the growth required in order to develop these attributes fully in your life. Unfortunately, many do not understand the differences between these concepts and do not appreciate the balance needed between them. For life to be successful and valued there has to be synergy between each of them. When life looses balance, it is more than likely that you have lost the balance among dignity, integrity, and freedom. The questions at the end of the teaching were selected to challenge your thinking and attitudes on each of these concepts. In order to live a life of value, understand the importance that each of these concepts plays in your life.

A Teaching from The Guides...

When man has ghosts within himself that do not always allow him to be the person he seeks to be, it is hard for him when he must set aside his morals of who he is. Even so when man lives long, it is important that he lives wise. In order to feed from the life path of which he has been given, he must trust the emotion that he seeks to express. More importantly, he must learn to be wise in the undertaking of what life is.

Man can choose all directions in the world that he lives. No one sits before him and tells him of the path he must walk. He is given guidance but he is not controlled by the world of the spirit. He is given choices so that he can clearly define for himself the muscle of his own abilities.

Man must learn the power of his integrity. Man is given choice in life to be honest and to be first in the way he demonstrates himself to those of others. Life plays itself out regardless of the tools of which he is given. In order to make the most out of his life while living, he has to place life away from him – he has to look at this life and understand that in it he is nothing more than a visitor that is learning to live in the vibrations of which life creates.

Man does not understand that life feeds him. He does not believe that his purpose in life is as strong as what it is. Man must know that as long as he is living here upon this earth, he is a visitor in the world of mankind. If all souls believed in that truth they would find themselves more well-mannered in the dignity of what they were and who they are.

For man to have integrity, he must believe in the journey that he has been promised. For man to have integrity, he must be humbled in the walks of life he makes. For man to have integrity, he must realize that in wearing a mask he lives a lie. For man to have integrity, he must learn to see his value shown to him by the sparkle of hope that he sees in the world outside of him.

Integrity to those of our world is to live honest from the root of your being. You see all souls take different turns in living life. Those today that you might see as your superiors are perhaps those that have lived weak in times of past. Perhaps those that you see in this life that live in poverty, that live in shame, are those that have lived once before with great honor, with great dignity, but they did not have integrity. Therefore, they have had to answer to a world that is foreign to them. It takes all aspects of them to live out this life, to find that seed in them that once again can be fertilized and brought to life. You see that is what happens when you do not live in the goodness that your soul is. You put out the fire in you, the passion in you. You suffocate that part of you that is true when you do not live in honesty, when you do not live with integrity, and when you lose the dignity of your own being.

To have dignity is to give you cause to create. To have dignity is to be proud of the person that you are. If you are not prideful of you, you will not live honest by what you want and need for you in the journey of man. You must learn to understand the value of integrity and if you do not live that, you loose you in the world of man. You do not live with joy. You live with sorrow and shame and you live hidden in the world of others.

You see dear one to have indignity is to not be confused by dignity. When you allow your ego to take control of your life, you are living in disguise. When you allow the mindset to be the ruler of your own world and not your feelings, not the part of you that is soul, that is spiritual, you live a life that is totally mental. You paralyze the abundance that is available to you.

It is important for you to know what true freedom is. Freedom is to live with hope in your heart. That is to live with integrity. The way you are, as you are everyday is achieved through dignity. When you have your dignity, you have your soul. You have your freedom. That is what all of you seek upon this earth. Integrity is the desire, is the want, and is the path to freedom. Live true to you by living true to the God-source within you.

When you feel shame you are not living true to you. You have caused harm to you. You must learn to live with less shame by going within your heart to find your spirit, to find the God-spark in you that helps create the cause for you.

Freedom--what does that mean? Freedom is having a purpose to your life. Living with dignity is when you identify that purpose. Integrity is when you live true to that purpose. Be still dear ones. Be true to you in order to find security that locks you into the role of life that you come to live.

Imagine that if you stood before the moon and the sun and you could choose which one you want most to be a part of. If you chose the moon, you live with hope. You live with desire. You live with promise. You are born in your world to feed the world with your ideas, with your original truth.

For those of you who chose the sun, you came to fertilize the seeds of which those from the moon will sow. Which role is most important? They are both important. For without one, you cannot have success with the other.

What I say to you is to know you were brought here to sow the seeds, to be original, to create while here on earth. For those of you who are drawn to the sun, you see this in the way you live your life...if you are drawn to the daylight, you are the souls who will spend your life helping others become who they need to be. That is truth.

All of you have been placed here to know you better. You are already who you need to be. You just have to awaken that part of you that is true to you and that is to have integrity. For only then can you be proud. You have your dignity and then you will be free to live with hope and desire and ambition. For this it is so. Good day.

YOUR INTERPRETATION:

_____

_____

_____

_____

_____

_____

_____

_____

_____

_____

_____

_____

_____

_____

_____

_____

_____

_____

_____

_____

_____

_____

_____

_____

_____

_____

_____

_____

The Guides stated during the teaching that we are visitors to mankind, and we must learn to live by feeding off the vibrations of life. How does this perspective influence your outlook on the world around you?

_____
_____
_____
_____
_____
_____
_____
_____
_____
_____
_____
_____

Are all souls, all of us, inherently good and full of integrity?

_____
_____
_____
_____
_____
_____
_____
_____
_____
_____
_____
_____
_____
_____
_____
_____
_____

How are dignity and integrity related?

_____

_____

_____

_____

_____

_____

_____

_____

_____

_____

_____

_____

_____

_____

_____

Humility is often referenced as a trait embodied by those more giving of themselves. How can humility, in the context of dignity and integrity, be better incorporated in your life?

_____

_____

_____

_____

_____

_____

_____

_____

_____

_____

_____

_____

_____

_____

_____

_____

Dignity and integrity are both important for growth and living a life full of passion. Both traits can also create difficulties in life when they are out of balance. How can this balance be maintained in general terms?

_____

_____

_____

_____

_____

_____

_____

_____

_____

_____

_____

_____

_____

_____

How can this balance be maintained in your personal life?

_____

_____

_____

_____

_____

_____

_____

_____

_____

_____

_____

_____

_____

_____

_____

_____

This is a powerful teaching because it does more than tell you the *why's* of living, it tells you the *how's* of effective living. Everyone desires the freedom to choose their life path and the specific route taken. Along this path, you are forced to make decisions, some difficult and some relatively easy, but they all impact the series of events that follow. The *why's* of life are no longer as important, but the *how's* of making the correct decisions grow to gain greater influence in living your life.

Freedom to choose and freedom to live fully are not givens. They are earned. We have watched numerous countries restrict the lives of their people by taking their own freedoms away, and this ultimately results in a society of hopelessness and negative conformity. It is not at the core of the human spirit, the soul of our existence.

While freedoms can be taken away by somebody else, the freedoms of life must be earned by each of us. This is a great distinction that is not as easy as left/right or black/white distinctions. Let us explain.

Freedom to live within the purpose of your life is earned by your approach and perspective to life and nature by which you contribute to mankind. To gain the freedom you desire, you must have integrity with your intentions and actions, for if your motives are insincere and fail to respect the integrity of mankind in general, your intentions will undermine the freedoms of others. Further, your choices will impact the series of events that follow in your life, resulting in more and more difficult choices. As a result, your own integrity to you and the integrity you provide to society will continually be tested. The alternative is to make choices and live life with integrity, consistent with the inherent goodness of your soul. It forces choices to be made that remain consistent with your intentions, in a perspective that contributes more effectively to the greater good of mankind.

It is easy for you to be consistent in your choices when you maintain integrity consistent with your own pride. Dignity is when you act, believe, and contribute in a manner that is consistent with the core goodness of you. Unfortunately, many of the examples you see in life are the stark realities of failed integrity, lost by a misunderstanding of their dignity. As a result, they rob themselves of their own freedoms in life, negatively impacting the freedoms of those around them.

When you live the life you believe, you truly accept that you bring value to others. You are a part of mankind, contributing the essence of you so that we may all learn and develop. So when you identify and accept your purpose, you must live true to who you are and true to the purpose of you. Only through this purpose will you live the purpose you desire, which is the freedom that you earn.

Do you feel that you are living a life of freedom? If so, how did you come to know the freedoms you are living now? If not, what is holding you back from feeling the freedom you desire? Is it a lack of understanding of your purpose or are you wearing a mask that is not revealing who you are to yourself?

_____

_____

_____

_____

_____

_____

_____

_____

_____

_____

_____

_____

_____

_____

_____

_____

_____

_____

_____

_____

_____

_____

_____

_____

_____

_____

_____

_____

When someone is struggling in life, it is important that he or she provide help to someone in need. Through this charity, they learn to shine a light on their own importance. Reflect on a period in your life when you felt lost and restricted but you were able to contribute to the needs of another. How did this action impact your perception of you?

_____
_____
_____
_____
_____
_____
_____
_____
_____
_____
_____
_____
_____
_____
_____
_____
_____
_____
_____
_____
_____
_____
_____
_____
_____
_____
_____
_____
_____
_____

There is a concept in human behavior called *Altruism*. In a sense, altruism is the giving of you without looking for anything in return. It is often considered the ultimate form of selflessness and charity. There is a great deal of controversy as to whether altruism truly exists, as to whether or not human beings can contribute to others without expecting anything in return, internally or externally. This teaching provides some insight into the role of giving to mankind as a whole, because it allows us to live closer to our purpose (dignity), with decisions made with the right intentions (integrity), with the goal to achieve our purpose (freedom). Since we are all visitors to this world and mankind in general, this is an important perspective to remember.

Discuss your thoughts on whether Altruism truly exists?

_____
_____
_____
_____
_____
_____
_____
_____
_____
_____
_____
_____
_____
_____
_____
_____
_____
_____
_____
_____
_____
_____
_____
_____

Discuss the feelings you experience when you give of yourself to others when they are in need, whether through charity or daily living.

_____
_____
_____
_____
_____
_____
_____
_____
_____
_____
_____
_____
_____
_____
_____
_____
_____
_____
_____
_____
_____
_____
_____
_____
_____
_____
_____
_____
_____
_____
_____
_____

Were the choices you made in this circumstance motivated by the feelings you experienced or the needs of the other individual? Explain.

_____
_____
_____
_____
_____
_____
_____
_____
_____
_____
_____
_____
_____
_____
_____
_____
_____
_____
_____
_____
_____
_____
_____
_____
_____
_____
_____
_____
_____
_____
_____

Altruism is a theoretical construct that is difficult to prove or disprove. It is impossible to discount the emotions and goodwill experienced when you help another. Charitable and philanthropic organizations exist solely due to the involvement of their contributors. Are these contributors participating in a vacuum of their own emotions?

Probably not, since everything you do in life have an outcome. When you help another, you likely feel a sense of accomplishment and reward for helping another. That is often the motivating factor when you help others. You realize that you have done a good thing, giving of yourself for the good of another. It is truly impossible to do so without experiencing the emotions you feel. If you did not feel something, it would be time to have your own personal oil changed for you would be a robot! The fact remains that you give of yourself for two factors: you want to help another and you appreciate the way it makes you feel.

This is not a negative, in fact, quite the opposite. The motivation to help another is an ultimate action of integrity and dignity, because the intentions and perceptions are consistent with your purpose in life. All of you are here to contribute to mankind, for the sum of the individual purposes equal the greater good of mankind. The true understanding is the motivation behind the actions, so as long as the motivation remains centered with integrity and dignity, the freedoms of you and those around you are maintained. That is the truest interpretation of altruism.

The drive to do more for others in an honest manner and consistent with the nature of you is the force that drives many. Each of you holds a desire to contribute to the greater good because you are ultimately part of that greater good. How you treat others, how you treat yourself, and the motivation for action all contribute to the nature of who you are. It is the dignity that defines you, and how you act becomes the integrity you display to others. When you live your life in a manner that others no longer question your motives because you are living in the right way for the right cause, you are living a life of freedom that is consistent with the life path you have chosen. To do it the right way and to do it for the right cause will be living this teaching every single day.

CHAPTER 3:
PASSION ... IGNITE YOUR INNER FIRE

"The purpose of life is much more than just breathing, it is about experiencing life.
Learn what it is to experience life, to have life, and to own life.
That is what you must seek." — The Guides

One of the most frequent questions we receive on our radio show, The Psychic and The Doc Radio Program, is what is my purpose in life and how do I find passion? While it is a common question, the true, underlying question often quickly follows it and the answers often provides the greatest impact to the theme of the call. That follow up question - what can I do to better live my purpose with passion? – provides greater insight than the purpose question. Purpose without passion is misdirected. When life dictates your living, forcing you to live reactively and in conflict with your desires, you are lost at sea in the ocean of life. It is all too common of an experience that makes it difficult for you to feel your passion and live for it when you are simply trying to make it through the day. Life is not about survival; it is about living. To *Transform Life into Living*, embrace the knowledge that you hold a passion in you that is ready to be expressed. In connecting with your passion, you better be ready to connect to your spirit, your God, everyday.

Open your heart and dig deep to find the fire that drives you, the passion you have for a cause greater than simply making it till tomorrow. Once you connect to this passion, the fire will illuminate the uniqueness of you and the desire to do more. This teaching will help you awaken to the passion within you, the desire to become the living, breathing expression of the God-like creation you are, without doing anything more than identifying the fire previously buried by the demands of life. Allow this teaching to be the match that starts the fire of passion within you, within your soul.

A Teaching from The Guides...

If man turns to the front of the book, he sees the proposal. If he turns to the middle of the book, he finds the plan. If he turns to the end of the book, he sees the wholeness.

In recognizing the worth of your needs and beginning to understand the glow of time in which you sit, it is through the instruction of your own needs that you must learn the buying of your power. More importantly, you must learn what it is to fine-tune the station of time in which you are in, for in doing that, you begin to find the harmony and the peace that brings to you. As you find the harmony within yourself, you look not at the clutter of you, but you look at the simpleness of what you are. It is that which brings to you the harmony that you seek, but it is the reacquainting of your own self that brings to you the strength of you, the divineness of you.

Maybe you do not understand the inner power that you hold, but you do know the mind of which you choose. Perhaps that is the most concrete thought that you can have upon your earth...that you are in power of your own thoughts. That, my dear one, is the fortune of your trip on earth. It is the spirit that is within you, the fire in you that makes for you the life you want as an individual.

As souls came into the existence of time, they were brought out of the cove of their union with God, but in truth all souls come from the belly of God. What is God? God is everlasting. God is power. God is humanity. God is spirit. It is truth that many say that God is the power of love, but what is love?

Love is an understanding...perhaps, but love is also shown to you by the ambitions of your desires. What is it that motivates you to accomplish, to embrace you upon this earth? It is the inner spirit of your being, the love of who you are, the love to connect to that oneness with God again, to find that part of you that is in the world of coldness and bring it into a world of warmth.

Try to understand our point this way. On a shoe that laces, it is the tongue of the shoe that keeps the laces from rubbing blisters on your feet. Well, know that the soul is that of the shoe, and the lace is the physical being, the body, and that the tongue of the shoe is the spirit of the shoe, the part of the shoe that provides smoothness. So, it is the spirit of the soul that brings to you smoothness, eternal peace.

How do you as individuals connect to that spirit in the soul? How do you connect to the fire in your belly? How do you connect to the sky that surrounds the stars? You see, my dear one, it is the fire in your belly that brings to you the most of you. Without spirit, you have no soul because it is the fire in you that makes you YOU. It creates for you the permanency of you. It keeps you focused in you and drives you back to the wholeness of the universe. Yes, there are times when the spirit is worn. There are times when the spirit is denied. But, what happens to the soul that has only the body but has nothing left within it? It grows hollow and becomes empty.

Many of you take advantage of yourselves. If you were to imagine that your soul is like that of the donut and that the spirit is the hole within the donut, then you could imagine the taste of the donut. The spirit offers you the taste of you, the true divine light of you. It is the God within the spirit, within the soul, that brings all of you together as one, that connects you to all of you.

It is not enough to seek to find the divineness in you. You must work to feel the divineness, the spirit in you. How you do that and how you live in that vein is to indeed know your intentions. What is the plan? What is it you seek? If you fuel the pot and yet you have no reason to want the warmth, it is wasted. Iif you fuel the pot and you want to eat from it what the heat provides, then it fuels you. If you have no plan in your life, you have no direction, no fuel. If you have no soul within your body, there is no reason for you. If you have no spirit within your soul, you have no cause of you.

It is truth that you connect to the spirit by getting in touch with the seed from which you bloomed. Yes, you have many faces of you that blend into the oneness of who you are in this life because you have lived many lives to perfect to the point of total union.

You are taught to believe that there is nothing in you that is more divine than the soul of you. You must know that it is not the soul in you that is the divine. It is the spirit in the soul that makes you divine. Is that God? Is the spirit God? God is all of life, but the spirit is the passion. It is the part of you that ignites you to where you need to be as an individual. This is why in this life you are connected to the passion in you, because you are seeking to find the spirit of you. When you think of spirit as passion, then you understand it better in your layman breath of life today.

What do we mean by the spirit? It is the passion, the personality, the voice, and the heart. It is the reasoning. It is the leaf that provides shade from the tree. It is all of that. While it is truth that you may have the body without the heart, there is no life. You are soul, but without the spirit, there is no reason for you. It is the spirit in you that connects you to the oneness in God.

What good would it be to have a river if there was no need for water? What need would it be for light if there was never darkness? What purpose would there be for food if there was no hunger? What need would there be for love if there was no reason for hate? Without the spirit of the soul, you cannot find the spirit in you.

Try to imagine what it is like in your world when you loose the teeth from your gums. While it is truth that there can be artificial teeth placed upon the gums, they are still foreign to the gums. You cannot become someone else's teeth in their soul. Your spirit within yourself, within your soul, is as unique as the teeth are in your gums. And it is that purity that makes you unique. How do you connect to that? You must know that it is the part of you that gives you life. It is the reason as to why you live. It is the fire in the engine that sets off the rocket. You can have a body, but without a heart, you never live. You are soul, but without the spirit in the soul, you are dead.

How do you connect to that spirit? You connect by belief, by faith. By having faith in you, you ignite the fire in you. By finding courage in you, you live by the spirit in you. By overcoming fear in you, you learn how to handle the spirit in you. So it is the faith in you that demonstrates to you the purpose of you. It is the courage in you that teaches you how to handle all of you.

It is truth that when you desire, you bring more into your life. But if you believe not in the desiring of what you want, you have no fire in it. It will not happen. You can speak truth, but if you have no energy, no spirit behind that, it will never be. It is only falseness. That is why you do not always succeed in the things that you think you should.

It is like marriage. If you do not have a reason for the marriage, a fire within the marriage, a desire within the marriage, the marriage will not survive. If there is not a fire, a need for the friendship, for the relationship, it will not survive. The spirit, the passion, the fire gives reasoning and you connect to that by having faith in that, by knowing and identifying the need for that.

Let us tell you a story. When God decided to create butterflies, he did not understand perhaps how to make them light enough so that they could fly. Have you ever thought about the miracle of the butterfly? It is ever so light, but how does it live within your world with such lightness and yet it does not have one territory that it seeks to find connection to? The butterfly moves very carefully and yet very freely on your earth. So how can that be when almost everything around it is much bigger, stronger, and certainly heavier than what the butterfly is?

God knew that he could not make the butterfly heavy or it would never lift and fly freely. God created for the butterfly a rocket, a rocket that would teach it to learn patience, a rocket that would bring it into its oneness, teach it about itself, and learn to create for itself the energy, the fire in it to shoot the rocket off. So God created the cocoon. The cocoon is the rocket, and the cocoon gives the butterfly the chance to find its strength, to learn about itself completely, and then it must find the desire for life, the desire for freedom. And when the butterfly finds the desire, the passion, the spirit for freedom, it soars. It is able to fly freely because it has found choice. The butterfly's spirit gave to the butterfly the courage to fly, to find its place, to respect the likeness of it, but to embrace the freedom.

That is what you seek. It is your responsibility to identify your cocoon. What is it in your world that allows you to drop down into yourself, to surround you with those who comfort you, to surround you in an environment that feels safe enough that you can explore and prepare for your freedom? You see, without that, you will never find the way to fly.

You must learn to have enough faith in you, to trust those around you as well as the environment that provides for you the shelter, the warmth that will help you become free within you so that you may soar, that you may reach the divine purpose of you as an individual. So what is it in you that serve as your cocoon? What provides for you the strength that encourages you to fly? Only you know that, and once you connect to that realness, then you know your spirit, the fire in you.

What in your life brings a sense of peace to you, security to you, and safety to you? Identify the people in your life that make you feel safe. That does not mean those that never disagree with you, but those that will always be there for you regardless of what they think. They will believe in your intentions. They will believe enough in you that they will honor you in the choices you make for you.

Look in your life. Determine for yourself who and what serve as your cocoons. Who do you want to spend time with when you have a need for energy? When your fire has gone out, whom are you drawn to? What do you need? Where do you go?

For that, my dear ones, is the spirit of you. That is the part of you that you must draw to, and it will always change. Once you strike a match, you can never strike it again. There is no fire left in it. As you grow and develop, your cocoon will increase in size, not become smaller in size.

You see if you find you can only trust a few, and that you want to hibernate from many of the earth, then you are truly not living for you. The more advanced in self that you become, the more broadened you are. The more evolved that you become, the more encouraging you are, for it no longer matters if you trust others. What matters is that you trust that you can fly, that you trust that there is a time soon that you will be free from the cocoon and you will no longer be threatened by those that surround you, those that have given to you the strength to find you, to help hatch who you are so that you may fly freely. Because once you come from out of the cocoon, you can never go back into it. You are free. Is that not what all of you seek…freedom, freedom here on earth? Good day.

YOUR INTERPRETATION:

_____

_____

_____

_____

_____

_____

_____

_____

_____

_____

_____

_____

_____

_____

_____

_____

_____

_____

_____

_____

_____

_____

_____

_____

_____

_____

_____

_____

_____

_____

_____

_____

_____

_____

_____

_____

_____

_____

_____

_____

_____

_____

_____

_____

_____

_____

_____

Thoughts and perceptions have a dramatic impact on the perspectives that you have on your life. Learning to be aware of your own internal dialogue, that voice that speaks to you during the day, is a valuable skill that provides a window into yourself. Like all things, the way you think is influenced by many things in your life, such as your attitude, your past experiences, your fears and anxieties, and your own desires.

To give you an example, when people are afraid to fly on an airplane, their own internal dialogue tells a wonderful story. Their fear may be grounded in reality, but their own thoughts and internal dialogue are not usually realistic. The true percentages of an accident become larger in their mind, multiplying the actual incidence rate to magnificent levels. As a result of their own anxiety, their thoughts tend to become more and more intense and catastrophic, leading to greater anxiety than they were originally feeling. That being said, the purest demonstration of the influence of our thoughts occurs when the plane begins moving. People who are anxious and have catastrophic thoughts become intensely aware of every bump, sound, and action that the pilot or airplane makes. They become keenly aware when the plane starts moving down the runaway and begins lifting off the ground. Their own thoughts force them to be vigilant to everything in order to determine if the plane will be safe. As they "check" everything in their immediate surroundings, they cannot help but find other things to worry about. As a result, their thoughts begin a cascade of behaviors that contribute to more and more thoughts of impending doom. Their thoughts triggered this series of events and resulted in negative and uncomfortable emotions. This can occur in many facets of your life, not just in fear inducing situations. Each of you can influence the perspective of you by your thoughts. Be careful of your thoughts and inner dialogue by paying attention and giving yourself the attention you deserve.

Based on this teaching, try and capture the thoughts you have about yourself. If you are having difficulty with this task, take some time during the day and speak aloud with your own internal dialogue. Record the thoughts and perceptions you have about yourself.

_____

_____

_____

_____

_____

_____

_____

_____

_____

_____

_____

_____

_____

_____

_____

_____

_____

_____

_____

_____

_____

_____

Our thoughts have a dramatic impact on our own behaviors. If we feel poorly about ourselves, this self-perspective influences our actions to be consistent with how we feel. All behaviors have thoughts that serve to trigger their outcomes. Negative thinking can lead to passive actions, fearful behaviors, avoiding opportunities, lack of confidence in life, and even lack of commitment to our relationships. Negative thinking can influence outcomes to be consistent with our fears, such as when people fear that their loved one is not showing the love and commitment they desire. Our actions in challenging their affection may actually come to fruition by pushing them away, resulting in a self-fulfilling prophecy.

These thoughts can be influenced by a variety of circumstances, but in actuality, we are in control of the impact they have on our thoughts. The pattern can be broken with your own influence.

Changing thoughts and influencing your perceptions is a skill that has lasting impact. Because the internal dialogue is always present, it affords you the opportunity to make the necessary alterations all the time. When a negative thought or appraisal pops into your head, you are in control of the fix, replacing a negative thought with a more positive perception. It is not easy, but the more you are aware of your thoughts, the more you will understand the frequency that they occur and be amazed by the true control you have over them.

Think about it this way – You would never speak to your best friend or child the way that you speak to yourself. To change the way you speak to yourself, put yourself in the image of someone that you love and respect. You deserve it. You deserve to be spoken to with warmth and kindness. Since you are in control of the tone of your thinking, this is the opportunity for you to make a difference in your own life. Divert the negative thoughts that invade much of your life to a more positive flow of energy and life image. These changes in thinking and perception will have the outcome you desire, because you will have created it. Remember, this skill requires practice and the commitment that you will listen to the nature by which you speak to yourself. As you focus on listening to the tone and the content of your self-talk, you will become more effective at changing the way you speak to yourself. If you feel stagnate in your own internal listening, evaluate this dialogue by journaling over time. Your own filter may surprise you before you actually put the words down on paper.

Apply these principles by re-reading your previous entry and find areas where your own dialogue could be modified to reflect a more positive and supportive internal dialogue. Recreate your own perception and self-image in the space provided below. If you have difficulties identifying alternatives, read your previous passage out loud to see if it is even true. Sometimes you even need to put it away for a day or two and then reread it.

_____

_____

_____

_____

_____

_____

_____

_____

_____

_____

_____

_____

_____

_____

_____

_____

_____

_____

_____

_____

_____

_____

_____

_____

_____

_____

_____

_____

_____

_____

_____

_____

All of these strategies introduced are important for finding your own plan for change. Changes in your thinking can lead to changes in your behavior that can be worthwhile and that can produce a powerful impact in your life, but it takes effort and determination. Unfortunately, too many people are lost without a direction to work toward and lack the drive to pursue their dreams. Your own internal dialogue can derail your dreams by falsely providing the evidence that it is too difficult, or too common, and by providing additional evidence that you are not worthy of the outcomes you so desire. All of these can be overcome if you strive for the outcomes that you are passionate about and believe in from the heart of your soul.

Passion is nothing more than a desire to achieve what we believe in. It does not require supernatural skills, genius level intellect, or unlimited resources. All that it requires is the understanding that we believe so much that we are willing to work hard in achieving it because of our own belief in the cause. We all have something that we are passionate about right now in our lives.

Many are involved in charitable organizations that require hours of volunteering, financial donations, and other forms of fundraising. Others would say their work is their passion, like many of the teachers that we know of today. While they do not receive the compensation they deserve, they do it because they are passionate about teaching the youth of America.

Passions change, and that change depends upon the phase of life you are in right now. Many mothers forego their careers in order to stay home with their children. Since they are passionate about their decision and cause, their decision will not create lasting conflict because they know they are working toward their passion. Other mothers work because they know, deep inside, that they can better serve their passion to their family and career by working and balancing their maternal needs. The most important thing is to understand your own passion in your life, because you must know what you are fighting for. In *Transforming Life into Living*, it is important for you to understand that you are an active participant in life. Life will no longer live you, you will begin to live life. Understanding the passion of your life will allow you to live life, transforming the negative thoughts you experience into the positive that you desire, leading to empowering life change.

Imagine that you have been given a FREE PASS to life for the next 12 months. You can do anything you want, go anywhere you want, or just simply be in control of your life for the next 12 months. The only rule is that you have to be committed to one cause, one outcome, or one passion. It may be helping a charitable organization, starting a new business that is consistent with your desires in life, or doing something for your family that is different from what you are doing today. Identify it...what is it? Please record your passion by providing an explanation and background as to why this cause is important to you.

_____
_____
_____
_____
_____
_____
_____
_____
_____
_____
_____
_____
_____
_____

In one sentence, please provide the reason that this cause is so important to you. If you provided that in the above exercise, please provide it again.

_____
_____
_____
_____
_____
_____

In your life as it is RIGHT NOW, is your passion achievable? If no, please provide an explanation as to why it is not?

_____
_____
_____
_____
_____
_____
_____
_____
_____
_____
_____
_____
_____
_____
_____

What attributes do you embody that will help you achieve your passion?

_____
_____
_____
_____
_____
_____
_____

If you were able to incorporate your passion into your life as it is now, what impact would it have on you?

_____

_____

_____

_____

_____

_____

_____

_____

_____

_____

_____

_____

_____

_____

_____

_____

_____

When you live life according to your passion, you are able to overcome so many barriers and challenges. We are always drawn to the stories of individuals who overcome insurmountable odds, solely driven to achieve what they always desire. The passion they have deep inside provides the fuel and solutions to overcome life's roadblocks. They do not see a wall, they see an opportunity to find a new route around it. When you live your passion, life is nothing more than exciting new routes for living. Unfortunately, when your thinking and perceptions become negative, the walls are too difficult to pass by and the easiest alternative is to turn around and stop trying. Learn from The Guides teaching that you must find your own cocoon to help you achieve your passion.

Living life without purpose is nothing more than going through the motions. It is no different than a nine-year-old boy attending his first carnival and not enjoying any of the attractions. While he may say he had a great time, he will never fully understand the enjoyment that he may have had since he never took part in any of the activities. Life is no different because you do not find your own spirit until you understand your passion.

EXERCISE:

Imagine a large fishbowl. Inside the fishbowl there are small pieces of paper that have a number on each paper from 1 – 25. You reach into the fishbowl and pull out one of the folded-up papers. Open the paper. Which number is on your paper? Subtract the number from the current year.

INTERPRETATION:

This was a year where your fire was ignited and you touched the face of your soul. You grew. What happened in your life at that time and how did it change your life?

_____
_____
_____
_____
_____
_____
_____
_____
_____
_____
_____
_____
_____
_____

This chapter explored the importance of finding your own passion and those aspects that may derail its achievement. It is important to understand that your thoughts and behaviors are related, so in order to live your passion with the behaviors you desire, prevent negative thinking from occurring. Change your thinking to positive encouragement and you will begin to live your passion everyday with purpose. Remember, if you feel lost and tired and the fire of passion begins to dim, ask yourself the following questions, "What/who is your cocoon? What/who gives you the strength to fly like the butterfly?" Through your understanding of the value of the cocoon as a period to reconnect internally, your passion will grow from the inside out, much like the growth of a butterfly.

CHAPTER 4:
MAN'S JOURNEY CALLED "LIFE"

"Life offers many lessons, but it is not the lessons that encourage growth. It is the way in which you apply the lessons learned that help you to grow." —The Guides

The first portion of this workbook explored the concept of life and living from the perspective of The Guides. As you learned, it is impossible to appreciate the act of living if you have no idea where you want to go and how you plan to get there. The critical understanding for success requires a perspective that every experience you have had in life has been placed there for a reason. It is there to teach you about the strengths, challenges, and resources you embody. Most importantly, to embrace where you are going, you must appreciate where you have been.

The current teaching shares a concept from The Guides that has defined our work for many decades, the importance of the lion. From the time The Guides introduced themselves in 1981, the lion has been a core feature of their presentation and symbology, both through their messages, analogies, and yes, their presentations. The Guides refer to themselves as lions, the kings of the jungle with the keen sense of adventure and hungry spirit, courage and strength commonly associated with the lion image. However, it goes deeper than that. The Guides are eager for each of us to feed off of their wisdom and courage for learning to live life by balancing the spiritual and physical demands of life. Like the lion, they encourage each of us to do so confidently. They are messengers for God's work, as are the Prophets of Isaiah, but we refer to them as The Guides, as they guide us in our life. They have a vision for each of us, based on peace, confidence, and wisdom, much like the ways of a lion.

A Teaching from The Guides...

When man starts the journey of life he is often reminded of the direction that he chooses to walk. In keeping that in his thoughts, he creates the element of need that is placed before him to reach the goal of what is important.

Man can choose many different journeys in this life path, many different journeys that bring to him the final destination of choice that he seeks as a spiritual being. What he must learn is that no matter how many times he tries to untangle the knot, the knot still remains until he takes time to understand why the knot was created.

You came into this life to simplify and to unravel the knots of heartache, just as you came into this life to celebrate what you believe in life. However, you become confused in thought when you allow yourself to be used up by the attitudes of other people. Therefore, you gain for yourself nothing. You loose touch of your reality, keeping you from touching your soul and being a part of the whole. It is important that you understand that to have success in your life is to live as one, to live as one in your own reality, to understand that this day you have a greater part of you in you. That you have the person in you that is best for you at this time.

You must not linger in thought about what you were. You must not linger in thought about the different aspects of who you are. Today live one with who you are and what you are. In doing so, you remove the separation between you and God. Know that your life is to be lived for God. In doing so, you live your life for you. In keeping that in your thoughts, you create a journey of peace. You begin to understand that even though the straw in which you drink from in life might feel clogged, you know that soon there will be another straw offered to you that is clear in the passage of nourishing you.

Today there is importance in the world about the wars and the conflict in life. You are fearful for the challenges that you face before you. You fear for the next generation and their having peace in their world. Your parents, your grandparents, and the parents before them truly felt the same way, but their own global mind was not as yours is. They were not given access to the issues of life in which you know. But they were given access about the issues of life that were valuable to them. Many of you have lost that in your world.

Perhaps as the world has progressed in time and the world of man has advanced in technology, it has truly provided him a pair of gloves that helps him defend the war within. As man creates this conflict outside of him, it is hard to understand the fear of it, to learn how to rest within it and not be fearful of what could happen because of it.

Man is given opportunities in all generations to know why it is important to live open to who he is. In order to trust, in order to know, in order to overcome the fear of life, he has to know the measure of life that is his proposal.

Souls in this generation will see earth changes. They will see the stars of the heavens become brighter and the world underneath their feet will become stronger. They will see what it is to confront the fears in their heart, in their world. They will see what it is to be led by strangers that are unfamiliar with the truth that lives within them.

You will find that as you live on this earth, you will see reasons behind things that you never understood; just as you will be baffled by things that you cannot even try to understand as to why they are. To live life upon earth is not easy. It complicates the world – even the world of spirit.

It is truth that the weathervane of life that is to progress sometimes creates cloudy weather. The thoughts are not clear. The ideas are not laid. The world is in turmoil.

It is important, too, that you want to live long upon this earth, but as a physical being you want to live forever. How can you stand before us this day and want to live forever in a body that is not you? How can you live in your life and not understand the meaning of you from an inner level, from a knowing of your true self? Did you know that the more distant you become from the core of you, the more fearful you become in the journey of life? It is truth.

It is not to say that all of you do not live as one, but it is to say that in mankind, in humankind, there is so much distance between the soul and the ego that no one seems to know right from wrong and wrong from right. This is why those of our world and those of many other worlds are becoming more recognized in your life.

You must know that the journey of life that is being lived is not the same as it once was just as the journey of life lived today will never be the same in the future. What is important for you to realize is that the tools of life that were once available are still available to you today. And, those tools are your relationships with each other. This tool of life can help you reach into the blink of light that has turned dark and not feel afraid.

Until you live one with yourself, with your God-self, you will never have the journey of life that was once promised to you. You will never reach a time in life where you clearly understand the meaning of all of life. What you will understand is how to live more open in life, to be more hearing of life, and to know the direction of choice that is best for you as well as for all.

It is truth that man questions the God-self when the world around him crumbles. The world around him crumbles, but man learns much as he tries to put it back together and he tries to understand the meaning of it. Until he is able to destroy the toy of life, he will never know what he has missed in trying to find something similar to it to play with it once again.

Life is more than entertainment. Life is more than a toy, even though it must be used in the same way as a toy is used. Life can entertain the spirit. It can entertain you as well as educate you, but you cannot run from the defeats of life or the wars of life for it is then that you show to yourself the seed of you, the soul of you - the core in you. That is the hope that we offer to all of you...to believe yet in the world around you even though the conflict of life seems overwhelming.

It matters not who leads your country. It matters not who speaks their truth. It matters not who walks a journey that is foreign to yours. It matters not about the world outside of you that is overwhelming you. It matters not. What does matter is how you understand your role in life and the instrument you are that will bring a purpose to others in life. When you live one with your God-self, you no longer question the purpose of your life. You learn to secure your life by standing tall in yours, by being proud of the world you have chosen to live in, by being proud of the voices that you hear speak about the power within the country.

You can take time out in your life to reach out to the voices that live beyond you in other worlds, not only in the nation that you live but also in the nations in which they live. In our world, the different worlds are the same as it is in your world. From this time of light to that of another in your world, another country, another nationality...you are as foreign to them as they are to you. We are as foreign to you as you are to us. The only difference is that the people that are there with you occupying the earth path have skin and they have charm. We don't always have skin and we certainly very seldom have charm. We are elementary with our truths. We try to help you become clearer with you. That is the message of us...for you to understand the root of you, to understand the oneness in you, and to understand that unless you connect to this part of you, you will never have peace in your life. You will always gain much from your life in materialism, in the physical aspects of life, but you will never seek and have the peace that you want eternally.

There are many ways to live one in your world. You have to succumb to the activities of life around you and experience them. You have to learn that through the practice of life, you learn how to still your emotions. Through the work in life, you learn how to overcome your hurdles. Through the joys in life, you learn how to be one with you. Unless you are to a place in your life that you are ready to find joy in your life, to find peace in your world, to find water to feed your seeds, you will never have a current in your life that feels right to you.

You see, there are many ways to fight wars. Man can fight wars with weapons that shoot him, that stab him, that cut him. But words are the worst weapon. Sometimes man does not understand how his language creates such hardships in someone else's life; how it pierces his heart, it pierces his soul. More importantly it cuts away his mind.

For souls who have mental disease, they have truly been damaged in the world of man. They come here to try to live once again for the sensitivities of which they feel are unique. It is strange to us that man is pushed aside for emotions, for the anger, for the tangles of thought that he cannot clear. It is strange to us because in all reality they should be the ones that man seeks to learn from. Their vibrations are high. Their energies are worthwhile and they cannot understand the vibration of the physical life. The chemistry of which they are is so fragile that they are unable to live within the realities of the physical world, the denseness of it.

Understand that what man has come to prize is not the truth of what is important. What is important is that he must have sensitivity. He must know and feel compassion for all in life. More importantly, he must learn not to be overwhelmed by just living life for if he over-reacts to life, he brings to himself a great distress. He must believe that he is here on this earth to strengthen, not weaken who he is.

It is truth that angels have a great deal of difficulty trying to deal with physical life. They are put in pastures here that do not feed them, for they do not want to eat from the grass in which others do. They do not nourish themselves in that way. They nourish themselves by serving others, by understanding the need of rewards, to understand the need of compassion.

Souls of our world create many lions within us. When we speak of lions we do not speak of those that roar in man's world. We speak of wisdom. We speak of knowledge. We speak of clarity. To us that is the lion's journey. To us that is what it is in man's world...is to be clear with intentions, to know the right of man and the direction of choice in which he makes...to question not himself but to stop living his life as though he is fighting a bull...to drop his defenses...to bend his head forward and to know that the roar that lives within him is constant.

You have to learn to hear life. You must learn to feel life. More importantly you must learn to be in life. Unless you are able to understand that, by taking responsibility, by opening yourself up to the roles of life and yet not losing yourself in the proposals of that, to stand firm with whom you are, you will never be generous in the path that you seek.

To be a lion is to be open-minded. To be a lion means to live one. To be a lion means to live simple. To be a lion means to live light. To be a lion means to live free.

We have brought messages to you on how to trust you, how to believe more in your abilities, but more importantly how to strengthen your connection with your God-self. We want you to ignite your heart and we want you to live true to yourself so that you can truly live with all. We believe that you must empower yourself first before you are able to understand the need for you. You must learn to look outside of you to see there is a world where you want to belong to know how to get to that world and become a part of it.

You start life from within; however, you must learn to demonstrate that outside of you to know how to honor you, to know how to believe in you, and then to become one with you.

We say to all of you, please pray for us. Give us the strength we need to encourage you on this earth to become your true selves and to learn how to live in a world without clutter, to be simplified in the messages that are given, and to be less stressed in your world and to know how to bring honor to those that have none.

What a distress it is to us when God has created such beautiful beings of light and you have lost that sparkle within yourself. That is hard for those of us from our world to understand. If you live in disease, if you live in confusion, you are not living your brightness. You will eventually dry up and you will create death and illness that is not yet needed. You must learn to know yourself by believing in you. You must see the sparkle in you and others, not the disease of you from the face of others. Look first for the sparkle and you will not notice the dullness. Know that if you look for the dullness first, the brightness will never shine through. You must look at your life as though you have lived your life long and that the path that you are choosing is one that is best for you.

We give you two words of knowing as we leave you. What we hope to give you is the burden of life that you carry, the joy of truth that is before you, and the journey of light that is promised to you. We will teach you how to live long upon this earth by keeping your heart open, and by keeping your words sane. We teach you that the most powerful thought of you is the words that you use. You can cut life up through your words, but you can also give life with your words.

Be aware of the power, the energy of words, and be understanding of the journey of truth that gives you honor. Do not leave yourself open to the criticism of others. Wrap yourself in self-love and acceptance and then the journey that others try so hard to take from you cannot be ripped out of you. You are secure within you.

We leave you with two words. BE STILL. Good day.

YOUR INTERPRETATION:

_____
_____
_____
_____
_____
_____
_____
_____
_____
_____
_____
_____
_____
_____
_____
_____
_____
_____
_____
_____
_____
_____
_____
_____
_____
_____
_____
_____
_____
_____
_____
_____
_____
_____
_____
_____

The Guides shared that the generations before ours were faced with many of the same concerns that we are faced with today. What appears different is that the current generation has lost the value of the experiences in today's society compared to previous generations. Examining your life experience today, what do you value?

_____

_____

_____

_____

_____

_____

_____

_____

_____

_____

_____

How do the values that you recorded differ from those of your grandparents? Challenge yourself here not to focus on the material values of one generation to the next, but focus on the values that embody the society you live in today.

_____

_____

_____

_____

_____

_____

_____

_____

_____

_____

_____

_____

_____

_____

_____

_____

According to this teaching, you cannot live as God-self until you stop questioning your purpose in life. That is a difficult proposition because it requires faith in the path you are on. Looking back at your life, journal a time in your life that you questioned whether the life path you were on was the right path for you.

_____

_____

_____

_____

_____

_____

_____

_____

_____

_____

_____

_____

_____

_____

_____

_____

_____

_____

_____

_____

_____

_____

_____

_____

_____

_____

_____

_____

_____

_____

_____

_____

While you may have questioned the path at that time, have your perspectives changed now? If they have changed, have they provided additional insight as to why that challenge was in your life? What was it that made the impact on you? Was it the process of having to make the difficult decisions in your life or the actual result, the outcome of the path you are on now, that made the impact? If the past experiences have not changed, what do you think you need to learn to overcome these difficulties?

_____
_____
_____
_____
_____
_____
_____
_____
_____
_____
_____
_____
_____
_____
_____
_____
_____
_____
_____
_____
_____
_____
_____
_____
_____
_____
_____

The lion has many meanings in our society and apparently has a meaning of great importance in the spiritual world. Everything has a representative symbol to us and the lion is no different. Describe the role and presence of the lion as what it means to you:

_____

_____

_____

_____

_____

_____

_____

_____

_____

_____

_____

If you follow the words and teachings of The Guides, the lion represents living free, with wisdom and full of intention to live life freely. Using this analogy, how can you live life without battling every hurdle in front of you and truly experience the life you chose to live?

_____

_____

_____

_____

_____

_____

_____

_____

_____

_____

_____

_____

_____

_____

_____

_____

_____

There are few things that you truly have control over in life. You may influence many things, contributing to an outcome or impacting the process of an event, but there are not many things that you have total control of in life. That is the beauty and the mystery of life, all rolled into one. This dynamic creates a balance of understanding and motivation that must be managed or you risk losing focus on what is important in life. When you feel you are losing control, the truth is you are losing perspective on life that creates anguish which you try and avoid.

While you may not have control over many things in life, the greatest aspect you control are your emotions. Emotions are reactions to life events and how they impact your own perceptions and attitudes toward life. When the experiences of life and those emotions begin dictating the interactions of living, the control of your emotions has been lost. Your reactions occur and then you deal with the consequences. Unfortunately, these consequences and the words spoken may have dramatic implications. Life with intent and wisdom require control of your emotions and reactions. You cannot live the life desired if you are constantly picking up the pieces caused by your emotional reactions.

Reflect on a time in your life where your reaction was beyond an appropriate response. What were the implications of that reaction? Did it help the problem come to a resolution quicker or did it result in a more difficult situation? With regard to your reaction, what resulted in more difficult consequences – your feelings or the words you spoke?

_____

_____

_____

_____

_____

_____

_____

_____

_____

_____

_____

_____

_____

_____

_____

_____

Were the words spoken consistent with your true emotions? Or, did the words spoken persist longer than the negative emotions you felt?

_____
_____
_____
_____
_____
_____
_____
_____
_____
_____
_____
_____
_____
_____
_____
_____

Was this reaction consistent with the image that you want to portray? Summarize your thoughts as to whether the emotions you felt resulted in the negative words spoken or if the negative words spoken lead to the original emotions experienced?

_____
_____
_____
_____
_____
_____
_____
_____
_____
_____
_____
_____
_____
_____

Have experiences such as the one that you summarized above changed your own perception, your confidence, and your own trust in who you are and how you live life? In other words, were you living and reacting in the image that you hope to portray? Please elaborate.

_____
_____
_____
_____
_____
_____
_____
_____
_____
_____
_____
_____
_____

How could you have conducted yourself differently that would have been more accurate to the true you – your God-self?

_____
_____
_____
_____
_____
_____
_____
_____
_____
_____
_____
_____
_____
_____
_____
_____
_____
_____

To BE STILL is to understand you, to accept the person you are today. It does not mean that you should not look to grow and develop. That is the drive of all of us. Instead, accept who you are and how you want to grow from that. The opportunities for growth lie within each of you. The voices of others are there for entertainment, not for direction. When you no longer trust the nature of who you are and the reason for your actions, the words spoken by others have too much importance.

Consider this analogy. If you are taking a bus load of preschool children on a field trip, it is important to know the directions to the final destination. If you have a map and have familiarity with the route, you will be confident in your decision making. The words of your colleague on the bus do not matter any more than a simple sharing of his/her opinion. In fact, if they disagreed with you, it will more than likely secure your decision in your own personal route because of the confidence you have in yourself. They may offer valuable insights into the traffic patterns and upcoming traffic delays. This information will supplement yours. The fact remains that you are confident in you to deliver the bus load of children that are depending on you.

On the flip side, if you were not prepared with a definitive route and did not carry a map with you, the stress of the experience would force you to lose confidence in yourself. Despite the fact that you have a general idea on where you are going, the concern that you may get lost and disappoint those depending on you would result in your listening to your colleague. As a result, you would place greater value in their feedback and suggestions than in your own, even though you had no idea if they were correct. The reason you place greater value on the opinions of others is because you lack the confidence in you. The fact that you get lost frequently or that you have greater faith in someone else may be the result of a lack of preparation. Nevertheless, the truth is that you lack confidence and faith in you, and when this happens, you begin to listen to others before trusting yourself.

How does this scenario relate to an experience in your own life? Did it turn out to be the correct decision? If not, please review how you could have had greater confidence in you?

_____

_____

_____

_____

_____

_____

_____

_____

_____

_____

No experience in life occurs in a vacuum. Understanding the interactions and importance of life is a key to living the life you desire. It is easy to get caught up in the emotions, both positive and negative, and forget who you are. You all have those experiences where you go through life and don't really understand the role being played and the impact on the outcome. However, the lesson is not to avoid those experiences. The true lesson is to understand the impact and the lesson that lies within it. Most importantly, understand that you are in control of your emotions and reactions and the impact they have on others.

Stand tall, seek the wisdom, and draw upon the courage of the lion to find the truth that lies within you. Keep your heart and head open to new challenges and new opportunities. Be curious and wise in your decision making, but remain confident that, like the lion, you are the King of Your Jungle, the king of your own life. To fully live the life you desire, take control, be thirsty for more, and be confident of the path you are walking in life. It is your life, so live it the way you desire.

CHAPTER 5:
IF I LIVED IN YOUR WORLD TODAY ....

"Life can become confusing if you allow the attitudes of others to take from you the journey planned. This will cause you to lose your own reality keeping you from touching your soul and becoming part of the whole." —The Guides

Imagine if you could look at life today from a different lens, as if you were new to the area and had no idea about the wonders and challenges of life. Would you look at life's experiences the same way? Would the details of life and the world around you have the same impact or would they be overlooked? The experiences of life are greatly influenced by perspective. Your perspectives change over time, due to life experiences, gained opportunities, or losses in life. All greatly influence your perspective.

There are miracles of life occurring everyday, from small experiences to life changing occurrences. Are you prepared to see them? Are you ready to experience them? Do you know where they are? All involve readiness to perceive, your perspective for living. Much like taking a picture with an expensive camera, you must be ready to clear up the focus, refine the image, and appreciate all the influences that impact that perfect picture. Your own life "blur" comes from your perspective so be prepared to focus and appreciate the miracles of your own life all around you.

The following teaching examines the world you live in from the perspective of The Guides. Unlike other teachings, this passage provides a unique perspective of the world from the eyes of The Guides with a review of time long before the time you recognize as now. Through this teaching, you will be exposed to a pattern of thinking that will challenge the way you perceive the world and learn to appreciate the details of the life you live.

A Teaching from The Guides...

In your world there are many complications you create all around you. Even though you look at life as a problem, it does not take from you the motivation you need to create a journey for yourself. You believe your life must be constantly questioned. That gives you heartache when you feel as though your journey is not as complete as what it should be. Your world is indeed complicated in the rhythm of life.

Many of you may wonder why souls from the spiritual kingdom are beginning to open up to a physical journey. It is simply because you seek to know, you seek to understand. While there are many worlds beyond yours, the calmness you seek is already within you if you will learn how to hear you. Through the wisdom of connecting to yourself and getting to know you, you will find peace.

In looking back over time, there are many planets of truth that have come from lost continents, and even though you do not see and understand the "buriedness" of past histories, understand that the plate of time in which you are enduring this day is exactly how souls endured it many centuries ago. In this time period, you must learn to disconnect from the emotion of the stir you create outside of you and center yourself.

Look at past civilizations to see what was taking place then that destroyed those kingdoms. From earth's early times, there were many pavements of truth that came to it. There were many rocks over the earth. Those rocks began to dissolve, to bring water into the world as you would know it, and to create more atmosphere for mankind.

In the beginning, there was no night or day. All was given life from the beginning of time, and everything was fed by the journey of truth that gave its own roots, its own source. There was no separation from that of the spirit world, from that of the other planets, from that of the other worlds. Everything in life seemed to have placement and seemed to run strong in the course that it took. There were no ceilings as you might think. There were no walls in which souls had to hide within. There were only souls that united as one, that came together in union to create a place of atmosphere.

Souls speak of the many creatures in their knowledge of religion. They speak of the forms of truth that have been given in the Bible, but many of those songs had already been sung long before the scriptures of what they read is read. When souls began to inhabit the physical earth as it is known today, there were no problems in the world of man. The only issue was how to fight determination in others. That determination was given as a source of truth that souls lived by.

Every soul had his connection to the "ethers of time." Every soul knew the importance of letting go and living within the volume of truth that was each and every moment. There were no rainstorms. There were no earthquakes. There were none of the things you see in your world today. All those things are here to cleanse the earth and bring balance and healing to it. They cleanse the clutter from your life. They change the atmosphere in which you live and feed the soul of Mother Earth. If you look at weather as the seasoning of the path you choose to walk on—as the spice of your own food, you will understand its value.

Man cannot live without nourishment, but he can live without choice. Man fights to find and have choice, but choice can destroy him and take away his world. Over time, man began to believe in his choice. He began to look not at determination as freedom, as a force within him that had to perform. Instead, he looked at choice as a difficult issue to handle. He was not given choices, and suddenly his determination forced him to face and make choices. Unfortunately, over time man began to create choices for himself that were not healing for him. That is when man began to fight battles in defense for himself taking more out of life than what could be put back into it.

Dear ones, that is exactly what happens when the earth is in the place it is in today. Souls have taken more away from each other than what they have given back. That is why many on earth are starved emotionally and physically. That is why souls do not know how to live openly with themselves. Souls today work hard to change who they are without ever going within themselves to work from a level of true knowing.

You can seek counsel or make rhythms in your life that seem to give you all the substance you need to live a long life. But if you don't know who you are inside, if you don't challenge your spirit, you will never leave this earth fed by the wisdom of time.

Many of you have lived in existences far beyond the one you sit with this day. Many seek not to bring forms into your hearts that create disruption. We are aware of that. But each of you must learn the importance of standing tall in you. The only way in which you can do that is to find peace with you.

In order to find peace, you must recognize your worth. You must want to like you, then love you, then feed you. That search will take you through lifetimes, uncovering parts of you that have been buried for quite some time. You must touch the hand of God that lives within you before you ever find peace in honoring you.

Why is this important to you this day? It teaches you about you and the river of life that runs within you. You must acknowledge yourself or you will not know how to live your life. When you are unable to feel the emotion of you, you are unable to exist in life.

All of you have had parts of you that have been taken away from you in the past. It does not mean that those parts need to recreate themselves around you. By going within you to begin working on changing you, you help solve the problems in your life. As you begin to change you and what you feel you need from you, then life around you begins to change.

Many souls live in such stirs that they do not take time to hear or get to know themselves. They believe that the journey they are walking has no rhythm to it that is sane. They believe that if they follow a religion they will find the God they search to know.

While that is the saddle for their horse, it is not always the hat for their head. They must find their own way of truth. They must live their own breath of life in them. The way to do that is to first understand the emotion that is tied to them. Souls learn to see themselves in a way that is peaceful, regardless of how disruptive they may feel they are.

You must learn to control your life by recognizing the reason for it. The gain to come from it depends on that. There is no time that has not already been lived, but even though the ground underneath was laid out for you in gold, every one of you has ever walked the physical earth has broken the gold that was given to you. All of you search to put that under your feet again.

Many of you speak of masters, of higher light beings. Many of you are that, but most of you do not know the wisdom that is within you. You look outside to find peace. Have you ever tried to hang your coat on a tool that is upside down? That is what it is like when you believe someone knows more than you, or you try to change them and not yourself. Eventually the coat you are trying to wear has no place to hold itself other than your body. That coat eventually begins to wear you down, burdening you. You learn to hate it because of the discomfort it brings you. That is what life can be like.

When you only live in the physical world, you do not see the reasons for the truth that is coming from each thing. You truly are the only thing that holds up the coat you wear. You finally realize that there is no rest, there is no peace.

Higher guidance is all around you, as it is with all others on earth. Every one of you has a God within you that is real to you. When we speak of God, do we speak of energy or do we speak of a voice? God is you. God is an energy that lives within you. It is the pulse of you. It is the electrical current that ignites you.

If I lived in your world this day, I would enjoy all the things life can bring, but I would never forget how those gifts were given to me, because I earned them.

If I lived in your world this day, I would bring pleasure to the faces of others just by noticing them, acknowledging them, and seeing me in them.

Transforming Life into Living Workbook Series

If I lived in your world this day, I would want peace for me. I would know how to taste the flavor of me by identifying my likes and dislikes about me.

If I lived in your world this day, I would value past times as though they were gold under my feet.

If I lived in your world this day, I would seek to know more about the journey in the world that you live, and I would learn to believe in the stillness of now.

Always remember that you live within your own jungle--a jungle many times filled with moisture, other times filled with sunlight, and other times filled with rot. Look for the reason for every trauma in your life. Find the possibility of choice that forced you into it. No higher being of light, as you refer to as God, forced you to struggle. You simply chose to create your struggle.

How can you change that? You can create more opportunities for choice when you begin to feel you have no choice. That creates for you turmoil and guilt. Understand the choice you make with every trauma, every joy and heartache you endure.

In order to find peace in your world and bring peace to life everlasting, you must learn to respect the choice of others. You must learn to understand the power that lives within that choice. Before you criticize and judge, be willing to open your heart to it, even for a second, because then you are giving blessing to it. When you try to take from someone their choice, their true freedom, you rob them of the journey of their own life. If you try to remove yourself from obstacles without accepting the responsibility of making the choice to have turmoil, you will only create more of it.

Taking care of you and learning how to live within you is a struggle for you, but remember, life gives you many tests. The way to touch your soul is to first believe in you, acknowledge you in all things, and know there's a divine plan for you.

When you are struggling in your life with hurdles in your world, it is because you are not following the divine plan for you. When life is hard, you are off the path. When life is easy, you are flowing with the path. Good day.

YOUR INTERPRETATION:

_____

_____

_____

_____

_____

_____

_____

_____

_____

_____

_____

_____

_____

_____

_____

_____

_____

_____

_____

_____

_____

_____

_____

_____

_____

_____

_____

_____

_____

_____

_____

_____

_____

_____

_____

_____

_____

_____

_____

_____

_____

_____

_____

_____

_____

_____

_____

_____

_____

_____

The Guides' often talk about PEACE. What does PEACE mean to you?

_____

_____

_____

_____

_____

_____

_____

_____

_____

_____

_____

_____

_____

_____

_____

_____

Using your personal definition of PEACE, how would you identify, create, and maintain that level of PEACE in your own life?

_____
_____
_____
_____
_____
_____
_____
_____
_____
_____
_____
_____
_____
_____
_____
_____
_____
_____
_____
_____
_____
_____
_____
_____
_____
_____
_____
_____
_____
_____
_____

The Guides state, "Souls today work hard to change who they are without ever going within themselves to work from a level of knowing." In a sense, The Guides suggest that each of us becomes so focused on making changes to who we are without ever really understanding what we are changing. Everyone seems to get seduced by the process of change, despite the lack of understanding what we are truly changing. In today's society, the focus is on changing and improving who we are, as millions of dollars are spent annually on procedures, seminars, and books to change our nature. Are these statements a contradiction? If you think so, please explain. If not, explain why not?

_____

_____

_____

_____

_____

_____

_____

_____

_____

_____

_____

_____

_____

_____

_____

_____

_____

_____

_____

_____

_____

_____

_____

_____

_____

_____

_____

Life is difficult enough without inserting our own commentary. Let's face it, we are not the best judges of our own successes and failures. In fact, we tend to place greater emphasis on our failures and discount our successes. Our failures tend to be analyzed through every detail despite the fact that the effort was overall a success. Think about it. Compliments are hard to receive, and typically when we receive them, we follow the compliment up with something we failed to do well. Does this sound familiar?

BOSS: "I want to congratulate you on an excellent presentation today to the client. You were professional, well prepared, and knowledgeable on the subject."

WORKER (US): "Thank you for the kind words. I just felt like I struggled with the introduction and could have presented the material better. I was so nervous that I couldn't remember my material. Oh, well, I will do better next time."

BOSS: "I never even noticed. Nice job."

We admit that this scenario is a bit simplistic, but we bet that it is accurate. Compliments are hard to accept from others, imagine how hard they are to accept when they come from us.

Why do you think that it is so hard to take a self-directed compliment? Does it mean less to come from yourself as opposed to someone you admire?

The truth lies in several parts. First, we are not taught to be comfortable with what we have achieved. The emphasis in society is to constantly improve, to grow from what we have completed. We do not allow our children to stop learning, stop wanting for more, or even to stop to enjoy the moment that they are in. In our society, our Presidents start campaigning as soon as they win an election, our football teams start planning for next season as soon as the last season concludes, and our book sequels are written as the first one goes to press. We struggle with accepting success and enjoying the moment. Compliments are no different.

Second, humans are naturally a humble species because we function better within groups. We are not solitary creatures – we like and need social interaction. Those who become self-centered or too self-enamored become ostracized by the group. Humility allows individuals to work within a group.

Finally, the critical nature in which we approach things allows us to improve. If we accept compliments without the critical review, it suggests that we cannot improve anymore. All of us strive to be the best person, employee, parent, and friend that we can be. We do not enjoy falling short, so by maintaining a critical review, it creates the motivation to grow and develop. Unfortunately, too many of us ignore the compliment solely to find a reason to provide the additional challenge to grow.

Compliments, both from the outside and those coming from within, should not be discounted or ignored. They are important because they provide the encouragement and satisfaction that is necessary to achieve more. If you have never tasted the sweetness of an orange, you will never know why it is so desired. Do not allow yourself to discount the compliment. Learn to say "Thank you" and enjoy the moment. Now, let's see how you do exploring the things you do well.

Imagine that you have received a huge honor and have been invited to a reception in which you will have the opportunity to share your views. Don't worry, we are not going to have you deliver a speech, but think how you would like to be introduced. The honoring organization has informed you that you must select someone to introduce you and they have to give a short speech about you and your impact to society. The association is nothing more than a "Goodness and Impact Society," a group of individuals that recognize members of society that have made an impact, both on the large scale but also on the small scale. The catch is that you have to write your portion of the introduction to make sure that it accurately captures the essence of you and will define the legacy of you to people that have never met you. Don't worry about focusing on the positives too much, that is what this talk is all about. You are being honored; make sure you make yourself look worthy!

Complete the following exercise:

Who would you select to introduce you?

_____

_____

_____

_____

_____

Why did you select this individual?

_____

_____

_____

_____

_____

_____

_____

_____

How will you be introduced?

_____

_____

_____

_____

_____

_____

_____

_____

_____

_____

_____

_____

_____

_____

_____

_____

_____

_____

_____

_____

_____

_____

_____

_____

_____

_____

_____

_____

_____

_____

_____

_____

What will be the reaction of the audience to your introduction?

_____

_____

_____

_____

_____

_____

_____

_____

_____

_____

_____

_____

Finally, I want you to write a thank you note to the individual that provided the introduction. Write it confidently, as if you are impressed by the introduction from the perspective that you are proud of your accomplishments but humbled by the humility of such an honor.

_____

_____

_____

_____

_____

_____

_____

_____

_____

_____

_____

_____

_____

_____

_____

_____

_____

_____

_____

_____

Take a step back now by going back into the teaching. This passage included a series of five affirmations from The Guides as if they were living in our world today. They provide a bit of insight on the perspectives of the world. Review each affirmation and summarize them from your perspective. Examine how you can apply them to how you live your life.

If I lived in your world this day, I would enjoy all the things life can bring, but I would never forget how those gifts were given to me, because I earned them.

_____
_____
_____
_____
_____
_____
_____
_____
_____
_____
_____
_____
_____
_____
_____
_____
_____
_____
_____
_____
_____
_____
_____
_____
_____
_____

If I lived in your world this day, I would bring pleasure to the faces of others just by noticing them, acknowledging them, and seeing me in them.

_____

_____

_____

_____

_____

_____

_____

_____

_____

_____

_____

_____

_____

_____

_____

_____

_____

_____

_____

_____

_____

_____

_____

_____

_____

_____

_____

_____

_____

_____

_____

_____

If I lived in your world this day, I would want peace for me. I would know how to taste the flavor of me by identifying my likes and dislikes about me.

_____

_____

_____

_____

_____

_____

_____

_____

_____

_____

_____

_____

_____

_____

_____

_____

_____

_____

_____

_____

_____

_____

_____

_____

_____

_____

_____

_____

_____

_____

If I lived in your world this day, I would value past times as though they were gold under my feet.

_____
_____
_____
_____
_____
_____
_____
_____
_____
_____
_____
_____
_____
_____
_____
_____
_____
_____
_____
_____
_____
_____
_____
_____
_____
_____
_____
_____
_____
_____
_____
_____

If I lived in your world this day, I would seek to know more about the journey in the world that you live, and I would learn to believe in the stillness of now.

_____
_____
_____
_____
_____
_____
_____
_____
_____
_____
_____
_____
_____
_____
_____
_____
_____
_____
_____
_____
_____
_____
_____
_____
_____
_____
_____
_____
_____
_____

Do not wait until it is too late to live the life you desire. Enjoy life as it is now. Take the time to appreciate the miracles in life, those experiences that are often missed by the complexities you place in your life.

Do not wait to pursue the desires of life or the appreciation for those that make you smile. Life is before you, not behind you. There are no regrets in living life the best way you see fit. Regrets only happen when you prevent yourself from living a life of desire, appreciation, and wonder.

The most powerful statement rose out of this teaching – to enjoy the wonders of life but to appreciate the gifts they are to me. Learn to appreciate life by acknowledging the miracles around you. From the flower that rises out of an overgrown bed of weeds, to the ray of sunshine through a rain cloud, to the smile on a small child's face for no known reason, acknowledge each of them and say thank you for sharing the miracles of life with you.

You are a miracle of life. Appreciate it. Accept it. Live it now.

CHAPTER 6:
THE PURPOSE AND MYSTERIES OF LIFE

"If you hold onto the past as painful, you will create it for the future. I want all of you to hear that because it is that pain in which you believe that goes with you in every day of the year. You must look at your past and all the pain of it, all the struggles and the hardships of it, as growth. You must see the good in it to see the challenge of it and to focus on the outcome to help support and give you new life. Remember, your life must be lived for your independence. You seek to find your oneness. That is the purpose...the oneness in all of you that makes each one of you sparkle." —The Guides

Life does not provide a GPS ("Global Positioning System"), the fun map technology that is becoming standard in so many cars, cellular phones, and gadgets. If life did provide a GPS, would life be any easier? Would you have a better understanding of your final destination in life, where you want to go and how you plan to get there? For a GPS to work you have to include a final destination. It is for this reason that a GPS for living would not make life any easier, because the truth is, you already have one built in. Many of you just do not know how to turn it on. Through this teaching, The Guides share their plan for making life more meaningful. Through **Silence**, **Abundance**, and **The Story of Life**, these mysteries become your GPS for life. Work the exercises and challenge yourself to find your own internal navigation system throughout this chapter.

A Teaching from The Guides...

When man lives in darkness, it is because he has shadowed himself by that of his past, bringing back into him memories of his yesteryear without learning how to let go of it, creating for himself struggles that he does not need to experience once again. It is of truth that in man's world there are many hinges on his door but the one that holds him the closest to his own past is that of his fear of letting go of it.

It is truth that in man's world he lives beyond the means of his own mind when he does not allow himself to work toward the humility of his heart. When man keeps himself open to the miseries of the past, he is recreating them in the future. Even though he does not understand the implication of that he still believes the need to wallow in it. This creates for him a sense of safe boundaries.

All of you have experienced parts of your life that you would not want to re-experience, and yet each of you think of that in memory as though it is a tomb in your heart that you never want to forget. And yet, all of you must work to challenge yourself by the seed from which you grew in that, and that my dear ones, is the part of it that must sting in that of your memory. Iif you hold on to that of your yesteryear in hopes of never creating for yourself that purpose again, you are blinding yourself to the gains that could come from your future. In keeping yourself in that blindness, you live in darkness.

It is difficult for man to look at himself and know what it is in him that is truth. All of life creates for itself mystery for that is the purpose of life. If man had never known happiness, he would not seek to find it again. But man must understand that in coming back into the physical earth, he has challenged himself by the logging of his own mind, by the memory that serves him.

In life there are many mysteries, but there are **Three Major Mysteries** in man's earth. The first one is **Silence**. Man does not understand the power of silence. He believes that in order to find silence in his world, he has to live quietly in life around him, but that is not silence. Silence is a knowing of himself without feeling the need to change who he is.

When man is silent, he is at peace with himself. He is in comfort of his own knowing and he is able to look at himself completely without fault, without honor, without fear. When silence falls upon man, it brings to him humility because he truly begins to see that in him there is a world beyond him. He cannot find the silence within him and not have removed the mask of knowing himself.

Man has many characters within his belly but the only one that is truth to him is what is about him this day; the circumstances of life, the outdoors of which he seeks, the placement of self in which he honors within him.

Without silence, you will never have any part of life that feels secure. Silence comes from vision. From knowing a part of you that is old and wise, having no need to change you but just accept you. That is silence. When you begin to truly hear life you hear the silence of which that is. You can then hear the voice of each other because you are not distracted by the puzzlement of you. If you separated your life in chapters, you would see that in the first part of each chapter, there is a need for listening, a need to be focused, a need to follow through with what you want for you.

It is truth that the second mystery in life is **Abundance -** *how to conquer it, how to achieve it, how to explore it. What is abundance? Abundance is in knowing your own rightfulness, what is yours and what isn't. You believe that in order to have, you must work toward it to acquire it. In order to have, you must ask for it with intentions in your heart of purity. If you believe you have not earned it, you will not have it and this is exactly why you create for you such war zones in life.*

For instance, if you believe you are not worthy of good health, you will not have it. If you believe you are not worthy of food, you will not create it. You must learn to feel abundant in order to be abundant. You must have abundance in life by creating a flow in life. You must look at yourself and wonder what it is in you that is not free because if you feel guilty for not exercising your mind, you will never seek to hold your concentration.

If you feel guilty about not exercising your body, you will create for yourself bad health. If you feel guilt in the food of which you eat, you will create abundance in fat. If you do not allow yourself to feel your sorrow, you will have more abundance in grief. Any part of your life that is denied will come through another vessel to show you who you are and what is missing in your heart.

Abundance comes from the heart, dear one, not from the head. The need to create is abundance. It is for that reason that you seek to have it in this life. What is the purpose of clothing if you have no body to put it on? What is the purpose of food if you have no mouth in which to eat it? What is the purpose of eyes if you want not to see? You must feel abundant in life. You must feel rich in heart. You must look at that part of you that is constantly scolded by you and then you will know what takes from you the abundance of you. It is that, dear ones, that you must see and understand.

The third mystery is **The Story***. Man creates for himself the story line of which he seeks to follow. He must act responsible in order to develop the story that he wants and needs.*

It is of truth that there are many story lines in which you can follow to get to the point of death that you seek. Death creates completion. It means on some level that you have acquired the knowledge, the experience in living that will give to you the next billfold of your own journey. But you must have the need to create the story for you. You are your own book. If you were to write a book about you, what would you say concerning you? What would you tell to others about you? Even if you wrote your own history and you buried it deep in the walls of life that no one else could see it until the day in which you left the earth, what would you say? Would you talk about your fears? Would you express your needs? Would you look upon your life as one that was accomplished? Would you think of yourself as being denied?

You have a responsibility to live your story. You came here with a story. It is your importance of self that must be found in that story. If you do not think well of you - no one else will. If you do not love you - no one else can. If you do not know you - no one sees you. It is important that you begin to understand those truths.

You have a story - a story to tell - a story to live - a story to pass on. Your impact in life will be shown to many beyond your life, by the roots that you provided, the anchor that you offered for those who you loved and adored in your heart and through your heart.

It is of importance that you learn about your story. What do you believe your purpose is on this earth? You already know. Do not ask us. You know your purpose.

It does not take you long to look at the falls that you have experienced. It does not take you long to know the joys in your heart. It does not take you long to find your feet on your legs, but it takes you forever if your feet are pointed in the past because you experience life over and over and over when your feet are pointed into the past of you, not in front of you.

If you want to know if that is the way in which you are standing, look at your life today. What is the message of it? Are you bored with the lessons in life that are given to you? Have you left the side of truth that was once there that is not a part of you today? What is comfortable in your fitting? What do you like about your life? What don't you like about your life? What do you want to repair in life? These are necessary steps in order to understand the value of letting go of the past.

Remember the past is important only if you can see the seed that was sown for you from it. What direction did the past begin for you? What did it create for you? What is it offering you today? Wisdom, pain, joy - only you can identify that. So you see, dear ones, you have a part of you that is not yet pure in spirit.

You must know that in coming into the physical life there are many things in which you must learn in order to find life. One is **Silence**. The second is that of **Abundance**, and the third is **The Story.** What is your story? What is the story line in which you are following? Let us tell you a story.

When man came to the earth, he looked upon the different waters of the earth. He saw the waters that had salt in them; he saw the waters that were clear and he could not find the difference. He comes back into the spirit world and he asked that of his teachers, "Why are there two different types of water on the earth?" The great teachers of time said, "So that man can remind himself of the wounds, the salt water, in which he still holds and the other can remind him of the clarity, the clear water, the sparkling of life when the wounds are no longer there."

It is your choice today. Do you want to live where things are not clear? The salt water is of purpose but you cannot drink it nor can you see the salt that is in it. The clear water flows gently and has a beautiful flow about it with its clarity and its taste of wonder.

You see water is the substance of you. It is what provides for you the cloak that you need to wear. Without water, you cannot survive in your earth. Without the need for water, you cannot find yourself living life.

There are many things that man questions before coming into his world. The first thing he questions is justice. What is the purpose of it? No one in our world will give to him that answer, because he has to first find the answer within himself in order to endure the life path.

Do you know the purpose of your life? Why do you think you are here? Everyone is given a past to decorate, but everyone chooses to decorate it differently. The past has no life. Why do you decorate something that is dead?

It is because many of you live dead in your life when you only live in the memory of the past. Yes, you can decorate your past anyway you want, but it is still dead. There is no life in it.

Why do you continually pursue the past when there is no life in it? Because when you turn a light on it, you see the gain of it. Therefore, don't decorate it with heavy ornaments. It will only pull you down.

Light it up. See the sparkle of life that awakened you to you, the seed of which it gave to you so that you can get out of the salt water and move into the clear water. Good day.

YOUR INTERPRETATION:

_____
_____
_____
_____
_____
_____
_____
_____
_____
_____
_____
_____
_____

What do you think your purpose is? Don't be shy or bashful on this question. It's important that you provide your impression of your purpose so you will be able to embrace the path you have chosen.

_____
_____
_____
_____
_____
_____
_____
_____
_____
_____
_____
_____
_____
_____
_____
_____

How can the negative periods in your life provide an understanding to your purpose in life?

_____

_____

_____

_____

_____

_____

_____

_____

_____

_____

_____

_____

_____

_____

_____

_____

How can life's purpose shift over time without losing perspective on your ultimate life path? For example, can the purpose of the life you are living today change, but the overall life purpose remain the same?

_____

_____

_____

_____

_____

_____

_____

_____

_____

_____

_____

_____

_____

_____

Take an inventory of your life at this present moment. Describe your life and your daily experiences with respect to your perceived life purpose.

_____

_____

_____

_____

_____

_____

_____

_____

_____

_____

_____

_____

_____

_____

_____

_____

_____

_____

_____

_____

_____

_____

_____

_____

_____

_____

_____

_____

_____

Do you feel you are living in a manner consistent with your purpose? If your answer is yes, what gives you this impression and why? If not, try to provide an explanation as to the barriers, both internally and externally, that are standing in your way of living your life with purpose.

_____
_____
_____
_____
_____
_____
_____
_____
_____
_____
_____
_____
_____
_____
_____
_____
_____

What do you like about your life today?

_____
_____
_____
_____
_____
_____
_____
_____
_____
_____
_____
_____
_____
_____
_____

What don't you like about your life at this time?

_____
_____
_____
_____
_____
_____
_____
_____
_____
_____
_____
_____
_____
_____

This is a difficult exercise to undergo, not because of a lack of information that it may reveal, but because we did not provide enough space to journal about the aspects of your life that you do not like. All of you are better at identifying those aspects of your life that are not working well rather than identifying those that are doing great. It is human nature to place greater critique on your own perceived shortcomings rather than to provide the encouragement needed for the successes in life.

Picture the dashboard on your car. Do the emergency lights come on when everything is working perfectly in the engine or when there is something wrong? What is the purpose of these lights? Do you trust them when they come on or do you ignore them for a better time in life? Much like life, the instruments do not light up unless there is a problem with your engine—an emergency. These lights serve as a built in protection against further damage. The experiences in your life are no different.

We expect so much more out of ourselves than we can often perform. Just like the warning lights on our car dashboard, we are more apt to say we have a problem when we really don't, just because the consequences of missing a problem are greater than misidentifying a problem. The _Check Engine Light_ on your car will light up at the earliest signs of trouble, even though the trouble may be minimal and self-corrective. Imagine the problems if the _Check Engine Light_ did not illuminate until the engine was already dead. That would be catastrophic. When the _Check Engine Light_ lights up, it gives us time to find out the problem and get it fixed much earlier and much less expensively than if it were too late.

Our lives are no different. We are trained to identify problems much earlier than successes because we want to control the outcomes and the necessary corrections. But, as learned in the previous chapter, we ultimately control our emotions, so allowing ourselves to get angry, frustrated, or disappointed with the difficulties of life does nothing but hasten an engine shut down.

The challenge for all of the exercises such as these is to take an accurate inventory of your progress and determine if any course corrections are necessary. They are not provided to identify areas of your life that are poorly managed or areas of your weaknesses. The difficulties you experience today and in the past likely provide greater understanding of your purpose than the highlights of your life, but only if you approach them with the proper understanding. By placing the proper understanding on them, you are able to let go of the past and apply the lessons to the present to succeed in the future.

Think back to a difficult time in your life and reflect on the experiences and emotions you felt during that time. Summarize that experience below:

_____

_____

_____

_____

_____

_____

_____

_____

_____

_____

_____

_____

_____

_____

_____

_____

_____

_____

_____

_____

In reviewing this time in your life, attempt to provide the purpose and lesson of this difficult time in your life. If you are unable to determine the purpose, try to identify the lesson by reviewing the summary you provided.

_____
_____
_____
_____
_____
_____
_____
_____
_____
_____
_____

What did you learn about yourself and what did you learn about your purpose by going through this difficult phase of your life?

_____
_____
_____
_____
_____
_____
_____
_____
_____
_____
_____
_____
_____
_____
_____
_____
_____
_____
_____

How has this experience impacted the way you live your life today?

_____
_____
_____
_____
_____
_____
_____
_____
_____
_____
_____
_____
_____
_____
_____
_____
_____
_____
_____
_____
_____
_____
_____
_____
_____
_____
_____
_____
_____
_____
_____
_____
_____

The experiences in your life provide valuable information for living the life you intend to live. These aspects of your past can provide understanding and insight that are often overlooked because your focus becomes punishing yourself for the outcomes instead of accepting the experience.

How do you let go of the past without losing the meaning of the past? You do this by shining a light on the past, understanding the emotions you feel, and accepting the realization that the past cannot be changed. With this done, you are able to move forward. This does not mean that the past no longer has meaning, because surely it does.

The past now has a different meaning with an alternative expression of understanding that becomes more aligned with your purpose in life. Your past, both difficulties and successes, are keys to your purpose in life. Without your difficulties, you may not have learned the necessary coping strategies and problem solving skills to overcome the challenges that are before you. Further, these difficulties may have changed your perspectives, influences, and expectations that have *Transformed Life into Living* with a more consistent purpose.

The aspect of the past that is most often carried forward is the emotions of the experience. As we have stated throughout this workbook, one of the few parts of life you truly control are your emotions. Since you cannot change the experience of the past and you cannot force a new outcome, the only things that can be changed are your emotions that you bring forward, but normally these emotions are suppressed from your understanding. Those emotions have tremendous impact on your life.

If you reflect on a period of your life with anger and resentment, whenever you are presented with a similar experience, you will invoke similar emotions. These emotions will continue to shape your experiences and set a course that is difficult to transform. If you are able to understand the root of your emotions and express the emotions that you are suppressing from that period, you will be able to put your past into the proper perspective. The challenge, however, becomes how to effectively express these emotions in a safe and constructive manner.

Journaling is a valuable tool for understanding emotions. It is highly personal and individualized; don't worry about the grammar, punctuation, and structure. The most effective way to journal is to allow free flow writing to occur without stopping to evaluate what you have written or expressed. The goal of journaling becomes the expression of the emotions. That is the purpose of this exercise.

Reflect on that difficult period in your life that you summarized above. Use the space below to express the emotions you feel today, but do so with one rule in mind – the end of this journaling exercise will have a conclusion that ends when you are finished writing. As you express your emotions and journal the impact on you, make sure that

you challenge yourself to leave the emotions on the page and not carry them out into your life. If you do not feel you are ready to do this, come back when you are ready and able to follow this rule.

_____

_____

_____

_____

_____

_____

_____

_____

_____

_____

_____

_____

_____

_____

_____

_____

_____

_____

_____

_____

_____

_____

_____

_____

_____

_____

_____

_____

_____

Transforming Life into Living Workbook Series

Let's talk about the **Three Mysteries of Life** that The Guides shared during their teaching. In order to move to this next section, it is important that you leave behind the emotions you entered in your journal. The goal of that exercise was to encourage you to express the emotions in a manner that allowed you to be able to leave them behind. Do not move on to the next section until you are ready. These emotions can be difficult to express and time does help the impact of these emotions. If you find that you are still struggling to move past them, take additional time to journal the impact that you are feeling. The truth behind emotions lies in the fact that the longer you allow your emotions to fester beneath the surface, the greater the impact they will have on your ability to express additional emotions. Take the necessary time to understand the emotions that you have expressed and continue to feel.

The Guides shared their Three Mysteries of Life as Silence, Abundance, and The Story. Answer the questions below about each of the Mysteries of Life.

The Guides describe silence as the knowing of the part of you that is wise, that is having no need to change but just accepting yourself. How do you grow without changing, by learning to accept you? Can growth truly occur without the dramatic changes that you often desire? How can your own acceptance be an aspect of growth in and of itself?

_____

_____

_____

_____

_____

_____

_____

_____

_____

_____

_____

_____

_____

_____

_____

_____

_____

_____

Acceptance of yourself results in humility when you are able to look at yourself without fault, without honor, and without fear. Then you are truly looking at you. This can be difficult to do. How will you be able to accurately and openly look at who you are?

_____
_____
_____
_____
_____
_____
_____
_____
_____
_____
_____
_____
_____
_____
_____
_____
_____
_____

What does your own mask look like?

_____
_____
_____
_____
_____
_____
_____
_____
_____
_____
_____

In order to achieve abundance, you must be willing to ask for it, believe in it, and feel you deserve it. Make a case for the abundance you desire in your life.

_____

_____

_____

_____

_____

_____

_____

_____

_____

_____

_____

_____

_____

_____

_____

_____

_____

_____

What has held you back from achieving the abundance you desire?

_____

_____

_____

_____

_____

_____

_____

_____

_____

_____

_____

_____

What can you do to change that perception of you to be more positive, more accurate in your life?

_____

_____

_____

_____

_____

_____

_____

_____

_____

_____

_____

_____

_____

_____

_____

_____

_____

_____

If you were going to write your life story, what genre/theme would your life be? For instance, would you life be a DRAMA, COMEDY, INSPIRATIONAL EXAMPLE, HORROR, MYSTERY, or a DOCUMENTARY? Provide the rationale as to your decision.

_____

_____

_____

_____

_____

_____

_____

_____

_____

_____

_____

_____

_____

If you are not pleased with the theme of your story and could change it, what would you change it to and why?

_____

_____

_____

_____

_____

_____

_____

_____

_____

_____

_____

_____

_____

_____

_____

_____

_____

Finally, does your story have a happy ending? Write down a happy ending that you would like to envision for your life in the space provided below.

_____

_____

_____

_____

_____

_____

_____

_____

_____

_____

_____

_____

_____

_____

_____

Everyone has a story to tell. The theme and ending is up to you. In a movie, the early experiences set the stage for the ending by developing the plot and characters and enhancing the story line. They all contribute to the story, and the beginning is not discounted simply because of where it falls. Life is no different. Your early experiences serve to develop you as the character, to set the stage for the events to come, and to enhance the plot in your life movie. Much like a movie, life builds to the big crescendo, the moment that the teachings and experiences of life reinforce your purpose. Do not discount these experiences since they continue to develop all of who you are and who you can become. They make life an award winning experience.

CHAPTER 7:
DIVORCE THE CAUSE

"To make the most of your life, learn how to erase the heartaches of your world. Understand the making of them. Know why they took place in your life, the purpose of them, the opportunities that grew from them, for that is the only way you will ever erase them. You will never forget the scars, for they will always be there. But the scar will hold good memory instead of bad memory." — *The Guides*

The previous chapter reviewed the **Mysteries of Life** with a focus on the importance of the past events in your life. To fully understand the path you are on, reflect on where you have been, not as a source of stress, but as a window into the purpose of your life. Life is full of lessons. Becoming stuck in the *Why's* only overwhelms the journey and results in life living you, dictating your perception of life without any regard for your experience. The *Why's* serve as the prongs that holds you back from living. Three little letters, but an immense meaning to the understanding what may be holding you back in your life.

The current chapter extends the philosophy that you must examine your past as a guide to the map of your life. Through this teaching, you will understand that appreciating the past is important for future growth, so long as you do not allow yourself to become stuck in the explanations of the past experiences. What makes this chapter different and valuable to you is that it provides a challenge to release the distractions of your past and fully embrace the opportunities of today and those that lie in the future. Enjoy this teaching from The Guides, entitled **Divorce the Cause.**

A Teaching from The Guides...

In learning to believe in the afterthought of your life and understanding the voice of your spirit, it has always been in the expressions of hope that you found your choices. It is through the direction of your mind that you learn how to believe in the course of what you must follow. As we come into the seeds of which all of you are, it is ever so important that you face the map of what you are on and following at this time in your life. In order to do that, look back in your world and see the directions of choices in which you have made for yourself even in the last three years. In doing that you come to know yourself and the gains of which you seek as an individual.

In order to follow the map, you must have an idea of where you want to go before looking at the map that you feel will take you to your best destination. You have come into this life to create less confusion around you. Therefore, if you do not have a map of where you seek to go, you will only create for you confusion and choices that do not feel like yours. You begin to overreach for the principles of life in which you follow. Nothing seems settled, and everything about you begins to feel smeared all around you.

When that happens, you have lost your focus. You have lost the map of which you are following. You have allowed too many distractions in your life to take away from you the path that is best for you. In order to understand the power of that, you have to understand the cause of what it is you are creating around you.

*When you are able to **Divorce the Cause** of all outcomes, you are able to see the purpose of your life. Many of you on this earth path believe that just because someone set a map for you to follow to fulfillment long ago, you must still develop that journey that would bring to you fulfillment. You have to realize that long ago you lost the cause of why it was important for you to follow that map. Many of you study that map and begin to lose sight of the glory of the destination that is best for you.*

It is important that if you create confusion in your everyday life, if you feel you are living in all the static, it is important that you understand that you have gotten off the map of which you needed to follow. Some of you on your earth create for yourself hardships just simply so you can distract yourself from the life in which you are living. When you are distracted in your life, when you are living a life of confusion, you are not following the journey, the map that you have thus far set for yourself. It is then time for you to re-focus yourself on you again, to get back in touch with your wants and your needs and your pleasures. And in doing that, you can begin to get back on track as to what it is of which you are seeking to achieve.

Many on your earth become lost in the confusion. They believe that until they understand the cause of what is creating the confusion, they will never find the destination of choice to be successful. While it is important that you understand the root of all problems, it is not always important that you wallow in that root, in that cause. It is necessary that you acknowledge the reason as to why life has taken you to where you are today, as to why life has brought you into the place that you own today. What is important is when you cannot get passed that, when you cannot believe that even though you have acknowledged the root of the cause, the difficulties, the joys, or whatever it may be, you then have to create a path back to the map in which you are to follow in order to reach the goals you have set for yourself as a spiritual being..

We want you to think about this. We want you to take yesterday in your mind. Look at where you wanted the day to go at the beginning of the day. As the day moved and progressed, think about it as you walk back through the day in your memory. At the end of the day did you feel you had accomplished all that you set out to do? If that is so then that is good, but few of you did. Most of you ended the day feeling some regret, wishing you would have done something more than perhaps what you did. In a small level of understanding, had you concentrated on that today, you would have felt weak and irresponsible because you did not accomplish your goals as you had set them early in the day. This would have ruined today. And that is exactly what you do when you create for yourself static in trying to always understand and focus on what created the problem instead of just acknowledging what was there to be created.

*It is important that you face the cause, but then you must learn to **Divorce the Cause**. The way you do that is to look back into your everyday life, to look at what you feel you are missing in your world today, to look at what makes you smile, and to see how much you have lost in that part of you in yourself. You must look at your life and understand the role you are playing in your own reality in order to get back into your life.*

*When someone asks you to become a part of their game, you either accept the position or you deny the position. Many of you do not either deny or accept. You exist. When you do that, you are caught up in existence, and you **Divorce the Cause** of reality. You don't have a reason to live. You don't have a reason to want. You have lost you in the muscle of living.*

The universe eventually will force you back into the cocoon from which you came. As the pain in life becomes difficult, as the voice in you becomes weak, as the path in you becomes cluttered, the world of life around you will force you back on the map that will take you where your final destination needs to be.

It is important that you understand that it is never a location. It is always a desire, a want, a drive, to feel successful as a soul. You cannot feel successful in any role you walk in this life, in any role you embrace, unless you acknowledge the purpose for it, the cause of it.

Past that point of acknowledgment, you then have to move forward through it and live the existence of the journey that you set for yourself. When you are unable to divorce yourself from the need to survive, from the need to prove to you who you are and what you are, or to prove yourself to you or to others, eventually you are lost in the cause and no longer seem to have any satisfaction for the fruitfulness that you can create.

So while it is important that you know why you have created what you have in your life today, it is not important that you wallow in it. It is not important that you continually bruise yourself mentally or emotionally because of it. You have to acknowledge it, accept it, and walk back through it. And the way you do that is to take you back into the lead role of your own life. You have to become involved with you once again, and begin to listen to you, to feel for you, and to become a great partner to you. That, my dear ones, is the lesson of our truth. Good day.

YOUR INTERPRETATION:

_____
_____
_____
_____
_____
_____
_____
_____
_____
_____
_____
_____
_____
_____
_____
_____
_____
_____
_____
_____
_____

_____
_____
_____
_____
_____
_____
_____
_____
_____
_____
_____
_____
_____
_____
_____
_____
_____
_____
_____
_____
_____
_____
_____
_____
_____
_____
_____
_____
_____

The teachings of The Guides often reference a "life map." Describe your thoughts on whether or not the life path you are on is predetermined or the role that free will has in your life.

_____

_____

_____

_____

_____

_____

_____

_____

_____

_____

_____

_____

_____

One perspective is to view the distractions and conflicts in life as learning opportunities, a chance to gain greater understanding as to the reason for the conflicts in your life. Another perspective, similar to the one offered by The Guides, suggests that conflicts only serve to distract you from your life purpose, fogging the clarity in which you view life. What are your thoughts?

_____

_____

_____

_____

_____

_____

_____

_____

_____

_____

_____

_____

In looking back at past experiences in your life, how have they served to hamper your ability to grow and be successful in new opportunities? Try and identify those periods when you felt that the emotions of the past and the concern over your actions might have limited your ability to be successful in new situations.

_____

_____

_____

_____

_____

_____

_____

_____

_____

_____

_____

_____

_____

_____

_____

_____

_____

_____

_____

_____

_____

_____

_____

_____

_____

_____

_____

_____

Now, let's do the opposite. Try and identify a period of time when the experiences of the past, both the emotions and the outcome, have positively affected your success in the future. Describe how they impacted your positive growth and provide the details.

_____

_____

_____

_____

_____

_____

_____

_____

_____

_____

_____

_____

_____

_____

_____

_____

_____

_____

_____

_____

_____

_____

_____

_____

_____

_____

_____

_____

_____

As you learned in the previous chapters, your past and the emotions attached to it greatly affect your present and your future. As this lesson shared, your ability to leave the cause behind and to focus on the learning within the past experience is the most important thing. Why is that?

When you live life, you experience emotions, interactions, and their consequences. Everything you do becomes stamped by these outcomes, regardless of how positive or negative they were. In truth, they serve important functions. Since you want to be able to remember important experiences in the past, they can serve to protect you, guide you in the right direction, or identify new opportunities that you would not have been aware of had you not had the previous encounter. These emotions and memories can be both positive and negative, depending upon the value that you place on them.

If you go through a very difficult period of your life, your memories will likely be associated with negative emotions, including fear, anger, apprehension, and even the desire to overcome difficulty. Those emotions may actually protect you if you ever experience that event again. The problem arises because not many of you actually encounter identical experiences again. In fact, not only do you experience the emotions listed above, but the more negative the impression left on you, the more likely you are to be trying to figure out the *why's* and *how's* of the event. The reason for this is that you become more and more emotionally invested in the experience and spend your time and energies trying to understand it beyond the necessary. These emotions force you to become stuck, to be stagnated in the emotions of these events, and to allow them to negatively impact your future interactions.

Positive past experiences carry meaningful emotions with them, and as a result, these emotions lead you to experiencing greater confidence. When you are confident, you are more apt to take calculated risks based on opportunities to grow and succeed, resulting in a pattern of behavior that allows you to reap the benefits of new opportunities, simply created by greater positive emotions. The main difference arises when the emotions of the past, predominately negative emotions, prevent you from living the life truly available to you.

As a result, the judgments and decisions you make are influenced by the emotions, learning, and experiences of the past. If these events are negative and you carry the negative emotions of WHY and WHY ME, then you are preventing yourself from fully living the life you have created. Instead, you are living the life of your past, trying to recreate and change things that are unable to be changed. Let it go. **Divorce the Cause.**

You must understand your role in your perspective of the past. You are in control. You are able to dictate the future. You are in control of your perception of the past and acceptance of the future, so choose the one that allows you to grow to the level that you desire.

Let's do the exercise given during the teaching. Think about your day yesterday. What did you want to accomplish yesterday before the day actually started?

_____

_____

_____

_____

_____

_____

_____

_____

_____

_____

Did you reach your expectations?

_____

_____

_____

_____

_____

_____

What feelings did you experience regarding the outcome of the day?

_____

_____

_____

_____

_____

_____

_____

_____

_____

_____

_____

_____

_____

_____

How did the experiences and expectations of yesterday affect today?

_____
_____
_____
_____
_____
_____
_____
_____
_____
_____
_____
_____
_____
_____
_____

What prevented you from reaching your goals yesterday?

_____
_____
_____
_____
_____
_____
_____
_____
_____
_____
_____
_____
_____
_____
_____

What can be changed about yesterday and what can be learned about the experiences yesterday? Elaborate on these experiences.

_____
_____
_____
_____
_____
_____
_____
_____
_____
_____
_____
_____
_____
_____
_____
_____
_____
_____
_____
_____
_____
_____
_____
_____
_____
_____
_____
_____
_____
_____
_____
_____

Through this exercise, you are able to see the role of the past and how it impacts the present and the future. The desire of many of you is to correct the actions of yesterday through your behaviors and thoughts today. Unfortunately, that result is a pattern of constantly looking at your life in your rear view mirror, and which hinders you from taking advantage of the opportunities before you. Bhrett often uses the following example frequently with the professional golfers with whom he consults. Early in their careers, they find themselves replaying holes in their minds and their dreadful rounds go on. If they make a high, unwanted score because of a poor decision on Hole #3, Bhrett can usually follow the decline in their scores on the next several holes because they continue to struggle. It often takes them several holes to realize that they cannot change the score on Hole #3 and instead can only influence the next shot that they play. Eventually, their own maturity and insight allow them to see the errors of their ways, helping them learn to put their mistakes into a proper perspective and not adversely impact their next shot. It takes time, but most importantly, it takes practice and commitment. Your life is no different. It takes practice and commitment to change your perception, to **Divorce the Cause** of the events in the past, and to recommit to living your life with full intent.

What do you feel is missing from your life today?

_____

_____

_____

_____

_____

_____

_____

_____

_____

_____

_____

_____

_____

_____

_____

_____

_____

_____

_____

What is your plan to overcome what is missing from your life today?

_____
_____
_____
_____
_____
_____
_____
_____
_____
_____
_____
_____
_____
_____
_____

What makes you proud of your life today?

_____
_____
_____
_____
_____
_____
_____
_____
_____
_____
_____
_____
_____
_____
_____
_____
_____

Compare and contrast what is missing from your life and what makes you proud from the two previous questions/answers. Which one(s) are you in control of?

_____

_____

_____

_____

_____

_____

_____

_____

_____

_____

_____

_____

_____

_____

_____

_____

_____

_____

_____

_____

In order to _Transform your Life into Living_, you have to take control of your life, take control of your emotions, and live life with the fullest level of intention and passion possible. We are often struck by the perspective that many of our elderly population embody. For many of them, their bodies and minds are not as sharp and active as they were 30 years ago. We would assume that they would be disappointed and frustrated that as they gain the greatest insight into life itself, their bodies and minds are no longer in their peak form. It is interesting, isn't it?

Often times, we see our elderly population energized by others, thirsty for the positive experiences of others, enjoying our lives almost as much as we can. Many of them have chosen, inherently or purposefully, to view life as a blessing, to live it the best way that they can, and to remain passionate about the causes around them. Why do many of us have to lose what we see as so important, our physical and mental capabilities, to see the insight that so many of them already embody?

Life is not about existing. That role is for houseplants. Life is meant to be lived. Imagine being able to give the gift of reliving the last 20 years to those elderly individuals who have the most amazing life perspective. Do you think that they would just exist, or do you think they would live life with everything that they have? Would they change their contributions to society, appreciate life with greater intensity, give of themselves more to others, or savor the hope they bring to others? Would they more effectively develop themselves and delight in who they are in order to give of their gifts to society as a whole?

The society we live in is charitable. Through a variety of philanthropic organizations, communities rally behind causes and overcome differences for the good of the communities as a whole. I have been a part of many charitable fundraising events, and many of us work harder for that cause than what we do for our own livelihood. Why is that? *Because it is our passion.* We are able to commit ourselves fully and to act with intent to reach the goals of the masses. We all have our personal goals which feed into the goals of the group, and that is what makes the charity experience work.

Examine your life as you live it today. Do you just exist in life, or are you truly living life? If you find yourself existing, challenge yourself to find your passion, live it with full intent, and divorce yourself of the causes of the past. Life is before you, not behind you.

Fast forward your life to a time when you are near the end of your life. Will you look back with satisfaction that you lived your life the way you intended to live, or will you look at life as if you lived it according to its plans? It is not too late to *Transform your Life into Living.* Start with your attitudes, your emotions, and your next action.

Take the first step by understanding that your past provided you with an understanding of who you are, not what you are. These past experiences and emotions have shaped your capabilities for success and no longer stand in the way of your future. Embrace the life you desire and live it with the intent and passion you would for someone else.

You are the most important person in your world, because without you living life the way you desire, you cannot effectively impact the lives of others. Take today and *Transform your Life into Living.* Do not look back. You are in the pilot seat.

SUMMARY & ACTION PLAN:
TIME TO TRANSFORM YOUR LIFE INTO LIVING

Transforming Life into Living - taking your life and making it live for you, not the other way around. From examining your past to understand the meanings of your life, to developing your purpose and passion in life, you are in control of the life you *want* to live. There is no one way to live life correctly, but there are many ways to live it the way that you want, purposefully.

The life you want to live is right before you. Through this workbook, you applied the teachings of The Guides and gained greater insight into the impact in your life. Each of these teachings has personal implications. It is always important that you reflect on the lessons to understand the meaning to you.

Over time the pearls of wisdom will only make more sense, so use these teachings again and again. The exercises attempted to challenge you and force you out of your comfort zone, to identify aspects of your life that you may not have examined before, and to illuminate the strengths from within. It is all part of the solution.

Life is a process, a journey that begins with limited knowledge and life experiences, but insights of the greatest magnitude known from a soul level. As life matures, there appears to be a waning of understanding as our life experiences grow and those soul insights become out of touch with current living. The goal of this workbook series is to reconnect the life experiences both encountered and pending with those of greater insight from a soul level. How we understand and succeed while balancing the emotions of life with the perspective of spiritual understanding is the meaning of life. Furthermore, and most importantly, that is the miracle of living!

As you reflect back on your workbook series, do not discount the smaller lessons, the ones that forced you to take an inventory of those that you are normally too busy to observe. Whether in life or in this workbook, those special experiences force you to reflect on the role you play, to appreciate the wonders of life, and to realize that the world of today is nothing more than a wonderful compilation of all of these miracles. Stop and smell the roses, appreciate the flight of the butterfly, for the wonders that it creates. Laugh out loud when you mess up instead of putting yourself down with criticism. Explain the workings of the world to a child and ask them to repeat it back to you so that you can see it from the perspective that your spiritual make up, your soul, sees the world.

Do not forget that you are the most important player in your game of life. If you cannot invest the time and effort to visualizing yourself as a successful player of life, you will never be able to be of value to others. You may help them achieve their goals, but you will fall short on creating the impact as a spiritual human being that we all crave to achieve. Smile, laugh, and be proud; you are ready to *Transform Life into Living*, because it is the only way you truly know how to live.

ACKNOWLEDGEMENTS

I would like to acknowledge my son, Bhrett, for always believing in me and in the work of The Guides. He has walked this journey with me, so he knows how difficult this path has been. I want to thank my husband, Jim, for always reminding me that the journey is never easy but always worthwhile. And, to the person who did not have to embrace The Guides teachings, but did so with an open heart, my daughter-in-law, Missy, I thank you. Your insistence that a workbook would be the perfect format for the teachings has been unbelievable. Lastly, I want to thank my friends and clients for encouraging me to offer The Guides teachings. Their hunger for higher wisdom has fed my hunger as well.

-- *Mary Jo McCabe*

I am honored to have participated in this workbook, as it involved every aspect of the McCabe family. The Guides have been such an important part of my life for over 25 years, watching my mother, Mary Jo, develop her relationship with The Guides into a valuable resource for so many. I want to thank my mother for having the faith in me to become part of her work, for supporting me in my decisions, and encouraging me to follow my own journey and walk along side of her professionally. I want to thank my father, Jim, for being a solid source of support for the family, allowing us to be free in our beliefs, and encouraging the pursuit of our own desires. To my wife, Missy. You joined my family with energy, passion, and most importantly, acceptance. Your vision for this workbook and combining the psychological and spiritual worlds will truly transform many lives into living. I am humbled by your support and dedication.

--*Bhrett McCabe*

Reflections:

231134LV00001B/59/P